Indian Management and Leadership

Spiritual and Ethical Values for Corporate and Personal Success

Indian Management and Leadership

Spiritual and Ethical Values for Corporate and Personal Success

Swami Bodhananda

with editorial assistance from

B P Mathur

Ph.D, D.Litt.

BLUEJAY BOOKS

An imprint of Srishti Publishers & Distributors

New Delhi

BLUEJAY BOOKS
An imprint of Srishti Publishers & Distributors
N-16, C. R. Park
New Delhi 110 019

First published in paper back by *BLUEJAY BOOKS* 2007

ISBN 81-88575-88-7

Typeset in AGaramond 11pt. by Suresh Kumar Sharma at Srishti

Cover design: Suresh Sharma

Printed and bound in India

Contents

Preface

True religion and spirituality should enable an individual to lead not only an ennobling and fulfilling life, but make him/her efficient and productive in the work place, so that he/she becomes an effective player in achieving the national and organizational goal of wealth creation. Swami Bodhananda Saraswati interprets the Indian philosophy, religion and culture for modern day managers so that they may attain excellence in whatever work they are engaged. As India, today, is striving to become a prosperous country and occupy its rightful place as an economic power in the international community of nations, an imperative need exists for corporate as well as public managers to produce and deliver quality and cost-effective products and services benefiting consumers and the common man. This calls for *good management,* which is only possible if rooted in India's own value system. This book is an attempt in that direction, presenting an Indian model of management.

It was my privilege to attend Swamiji's lectures in various management forums, tape-record them, have them transcribed and then edit the transcripts to create a readable format. Swamiji has extensively re-edited the lectures and has presented a consistent and comprehensive philosophy of Indian thought in management. The advantage in presenting the book in lecture format is that the reader gets a feeling that he/she is in dialogue with Swamiji, in the traditional *guru shishya parampara*. The book, while discussing 'Indian Ethos' in management, extensively covers themes of leadership and global competition—major concerns of the modern manager. In the epilogue, 'Ten Spiritual Principles of Indian Management', Swamiji enunciates the relevance of Indian wisdom, tradition and culture for the

Indian manager. Swamiji rightly mentions that the modern-day Indian manager is caught between the materialist values of modern age and the spiritual values of our ancient culture. On one hand he/she is asked to produce wealth and promote culture of consumerism and on the other side, he/she is told that wealth is evil and he/she should practice "desire-less-ness." This cleavage confuses the manager and leaves a chasm in his/her soul. Swamiji, through his deep insight of the Vedanta and Indian scriptures as well as profound understanding of Western scientific thought, reconciles the two seemingly opposing viewpoints and presents a model of management, which, while rooted in Indian wisdom and tradition, embraces the salient features of modern management theory.

I would like to express my deep gratitude to Sangeetha Menon, Senior Fellow, National Institute of Advanced Studies, who with her deep knowledge of Sanskrit and Indian scriptures has been a valuable guide and collaborator in bringing out this book. I also acknowledge the assistance given by Paul Janson, of Sambodh Society (USA), whose computer formatting expertise facilitated the editorial work. I also express my thanks to the All India Management Association, New Delhi; Department of Management Studies, IIT, New Delhi; University Business School, Punjab University, and Senior Citizen Council for HRD, Chandigarh; Indian Institute of Public Administration, New Delhi, and other management forums, for inviting Swami Bodhananda Saraswati for lectures and engaging in enlightened discussion with Swamiji, all of which facilitated production of this book. JK Bose of Srishti Publishers has done commendable work in bringing out this publication as well as Swami Bodhananda's other publications, helping to spread Swamiji's noble message across the country.

Sambodh Foundation, under whose auspices this book has been published, will be happy to have a continuing dialogue with its readers, practicing managers, academicians and others interested in the subject, who hold a view to develop an Indian model of management suited to the genius of our country.

Dashehra, October 2, 2006

Birendra Prasad Mathur

Website: www.sambodh.org
www.sambodh.com

Email: info@sambodh.org
swami_bodhananda@charter.net

Introducing the Book

B P Mathur

India today stands at the threshold of a great destiny. It has shed its accumulated inertia of the past and is emerging as an economic power. India is now the fourth largest economy in the world in terms of PPP, ahead of Germany and UK. Indian companies are becoming global players, across large industrial segments such as automobile, pharmaceuticals, and textiles. In Information Technology (IT) India has emerged as a world leader. The outsourcing of software services to India has raised a huge outcry in US and European countries as it is leading to loss of white collared jobs. The famed Silicon Valley of USA is dotted with the presence of Indian engineers and technicians at the cutting edge of technology. The Indian success in IT has given a new self-confidence to the nation and a sense of national pride that we can compete with the best in the world. Futurologists predict that in another 25 years India has the potential of becoming the third largest economy in the world, in real dollar terms, overtaking Japan. Can we fulfill this prophecy? While India's achievements are laudable, our record on social front is deplorable. India is one of the poorest countries in the world, with 25 percent of people living in abject poverty and another 50 percent barely eking out a living. One-third Indians are illiterate and have no access even to primary health services. How do we pull out our people from the clutches of poverty and deprivation and give them a dignified living? This is a huge challenge facing the country. I would say a huge management challenge.

The problem with India is not lack of resources. In fact, India is a resource rich country with plenty of sunshine, rains, water, minerals and forest wealth. India's problem again, is not lack of enterprise on the part of people. Indians, who had gone as indentured laborers to Mauritius, Fiji, and Guyana a century back, today hold the reins of economic and political power in the countries of their adoption. The Indian presence in USA and UK stretches from the highest echelons in corporate and business world to the most prestigious universities and research labs inviting respect of the international community. The problem of India is basically a problem of management—management of its vast pool of manpower.

Basic Foundation of Management

Management basically means managing human beings. The management guru, Peter Drucker, says that management's task is to make people capable of joint performance and make their strength effective. Management is about action. When people are motivated and inspired they run their organizations efficiently and profitably, produce quality goods and services, and keep customers and clients satisfied. Management is deeply embedded in culture. Across all cultures and in all societies, human beings coming together to perform certain collective tasks encounter common problems related to establishing direction, coordination and motivation. Culture affects how these problems are perceived and how they are resolved. That is why we say the American or the Japanese or the German style of management. What does that mean? Is there something like Indian style of management? Can we describe its basic characteristics and develop a theory about Indian style of management? Today Indian industry has come of age and is making successful forays in the international market. Indian firms such as Tata Group, Ranbaxy, Bharat

Forge, have set up or acquired firms abroad and are running them successfully. Is there some common thread amongst them which make them distinctive, say from a Chinese or a Korean firm?

Takeo Fujiswa[1] founder of the Honda Motor Company observes, "*Japanese and American management is 95 percent the same and differs in all important aspects.*" Much the same can be said about Indian management. After all, basic principles of management are the same all over the world. It is the details that make a difference and help to develop a distinctive style for every country or firm. Some commentary on the style of management of some of the most successful economies will help us better understand the issue.

Matsushita a global giant in electrical and electronics reflects typically Japanese style of management. Its philosophy provides a basis of meaning beyond the product it produces. The firm feels that the company has a responsibility to help the employees' inner-self. This can be realized by tying the company and the individual by insisting that management serves as trainers and developers of character, not just exploiters of human resources. Its *Basic Business Principles* are: To recognize our responsibilities as industrialists, to foster progress, to promote the general welfare of society, and to devote ourselves to the further development of world culture. Its *Seven Spiritual Values* are: 1) National Service Through Industry, 2) Fairness, 3) Harmony and Cooperation, 4) Struggle for Betterment, 5) Courtesy and Humility, 6) Adjustment and Assimilation, 7) Gratitude. Matsushita, interweaving human values with hard edge

[1]Richard Pascale and Anthony Athos: The Art of Japanese Management, (Penguin Books, New York, 1983), p 85

efficiency, has created an organization of astonishing resilience and efficiency.

Tom Peters and Robert Waterman in their classic *In search of Excellence* lay down eight basic principles, which can be treated as basic ingredients of American style of management: a bias for action; staying close to customer; autonomy and entrepreneurship; productivity through people; hands-on value driven; stick to knitting; simple form – lean staff; and simultaneous loose-tight properties. Successful companies regard people as the most important asset and are organized to obtain extraordinary effort from ordinary people. Excellent companies have deeply ingrained philosophy of respecting the individual and making people winners. An important characteristic of a successful venture is its value system. Thomas Watson[2] founder of IBM observed, 'the basic philosophy, spirit and drive of an organization have far more to do with its relative achievements than do technological or economic resources, organizational structure, innovation and timing.' Watson mentions three sets of beliefs: 1) Respect for the Individual. Respect for the dignity and rights for each person in the organization. 2) Customer service. To give the best customer service of any company in the world. 3) Excellence. The conviction that an organization should pursue all tasks with the object of accomplishing them in a superior way.

Religion and Management Values

Religion has played an important role in shaping management values in the rich societies. In USA, UK, Germany, largely

[2] Pascale and Ethos *ibid*, p 184

protestant countries, the meaning of work was radically altered by Protestant ethics which preached salvation through work instead of salvation by faith. The Calvinists converted hard work, honesty, seriousness, the proper use of time and money, as secular code of behaviour. Max Weber in his *Protestant Ethics and the Spirit of Capitalism* and R H Tawney in *Religion and Rise of Capitalism* have pointed out the important role played by Protestant ethics in economic success of Western societies. Japanese have been profoundly influenced by Buddhism. According to Buddhism, the function of work is threefold: to enable a person to develop himself; to make him aware of the need to help others; to produce goods and services needed for a meaningful existence. Zen Buddhism holds that all work is sacred. Japanese culture defines an individual entirely in terms of others and induces people to work towards achievement of the goals of the organization.

Indian Culture and Management

Management is basically rooted in the culture of a society. When we talk of Indian ethos in management what does it mean? What do we mean by Indian wisdom and tradition? Is there something like Indian culture? When we talk of Indian wisdom and tradition, it basically implies *Vedantic* thought as expressed in *Bhagawad Gita*, which contains the essence of Upanishads. The traditional Indian wisdom is also known as *sanatana dharma*, which has found its most profound expression in the great epic *Ramayana*, related in a story form for the understanding of the common man. While there may be divergent religious practices amongst people living in North, South, East and West India and also amongst different communities and sects living in the same geographical location, they all derive their inspiration from the teachings of Vedanta.

SK Chakraborty[3] gives a beautiful metaphor to describe what he calls the *Yoga- Vedantic* tradition as the key component of Indian wisdom and culture. A beautiful necklace is a composite of many gems but it is one pendant which is the center-piece, the largest, the brightest and most precious around which all the gems are strung. The indigenous religions, Buddhism, Jainism, Sikhism and the various sects of Hindu religion all derive their inspiration from the central philosophy of Vedanta. Thus while Indian culture is a vast mosaic of many gems, they are embedded around the central piece of *Vedantic* philosophy. If you travel any where in India, from East to West and from North to South, during a festival season such as Dashera-Dewali, you see people celebrating with gay abandon, *Durga-puja* in West Bengal, *garba dance* in Gujarat, *Ramlila* in Uttar Pradesh and *Deepawali* in Tamilnadu, all dedicated at the altar of some higher power, underscoring the religious and cultural unity of our ancient civilization.

India is a pluralistic society with large Muslim and Christian population. India's religious tradition gives space to every religion to search God and the Truth in its own way. This is expressed in one of the great *vedic* verses: *Ekam sad vipra bahuda vadanti*- 'the Truth is one, sages call it by various names'. Our great saints aver that Vedas are the knowledge of all Indians, in fact of whole humanity, and not only of people practicing Hinduism. Just as Sufism cannot be said to belong only to the Muslims or the Bible to the Christians but to the whole humanity, Vedanta is a

---

[3] S K Chakraborty : Against the Tide: The Philosophical Foundations of Modern Management, (Oxford, New Delhi, 2003), pp. 200-205

heritage of the mankind. Thus every Indian should feel a sense of belonging to all that is Indian, including language, literature and spirituality.

Gita and its Appeal to the Man of Action

The essence of Indian wisdom and philosophy is most succinctly expressed in *Bhagawad Gita – The Song Celestial.* Gita's philosophy has appealed and influenced the great minds of the Western world such as Ralph Waldo Emerson, Albert Schweitzer and Albert Einstein. Aldous Huxley said, "The Gita is one of the clearest and the most comprehensive summaries of the perennial philosophy ever to have been made. Hence it has enduring value, not only for the Indians but for the mankind." Mahatma Gandhi[4] described Gita as his mother and observed, " I lost my earthly mother who gave me birth long ago, but this eternal mother has completely filled her place by my side ever since. She has never changed, she has never failed. When I am in difficulty or distress, I seek refuge in her bosom." Gita provides wisdom and upliftment, comfort and solace to people of all ages, from all walks of life, from all corners of the world. Gita describes three paths of *karm-yog, bhakti-yog and gyan-yog* to realize the Truth and achieve life's purpose. While the three paths are not mutually exclusive, it is the *karm-yog* which is of particular relevance to the modern man of 'action' living in a turbulent world. The message of the Gita is to perform your duties diligently and piously, but without any expectation of what the results will be. You must till the soil, plant the seeds, water and tend the seedling, and take care of the tree, without any thought

[4] Jag Pravesh Chander (ed): Gita the Mother, (Indian Printing works, Lahore, 1946-47), p. 5

of how much fruit the tree will bear. Expectation is the mother of frustration, but acceptance is the mother of peace and joy. Life is about the journey, not the destination. Gita's *karmyoga* message has the most telling appeal to leaders and movers of society, top managers and administrators and all those engaged in pursuit of earning a righteous living, where they have to face the battle of life, accept the challenge, struggle and keep marching onwards.

Swami Bodhananda's Management Thoughts

This book presents Swami Bodhananda's lectures on Indian Ethos in Management delivered to corporate managers and public administrators at various forums such as All India Management Association, IIT Delhi, Panjab University Chandigarh, Indian Institute of Public Administration, etc. Swami Bodhananda is a great scholar of Vedanta and an enlightened *sanyasi*. With his erudition and deep insight of ancient scriptures, he combines in himself rational and mystic qualities which make him a captivating and engaging public speaker. In a series of lectures such as personality re-engineering, *guna* analysis, work culture and *yajna-tradition*, leadership, cultural values, Swamiji points out how our ancient wisdom and tradition can inspire and motivate managers and public administrators to attain *excellence* in whatever they do. Swamiji is no blind follower of ancient wisdom. He is a ruthless critic too. He says, that we must have the courage to critique our past and interpret and adapt it to the modern needs. He feels that part of ancient thought, which does not harmonise with modern values of democracy, secularism and equality, should be ruthlessly discarded. Swamiji asserts that the role of spirituality is to create competent and effective managers. Spirituality has to be practiced in daily life and in action and not in the caves of Himalayas. Swamiji gives a unique interpretation of *desirelessness* as enunciated in Vedanta. According to him *desirelessness* means, 'to give and to share'. Swamiji extols the virtues of wealth creation and argues that it is not only a perfectly legitimate activity, but is the foremost duty of every Indian. One should engage in the activity of wealth creation, but with a spirit of *detached engagement.*

India is today struggling to break the poverty trap and become a prosperous society and occupy a rightful place in international comity of nations. We need ignited minds to make India a wealthy country both materially and spiritually where people are above basic want of day-to-day living, live in harmony and pursue a *dharmic* code of conduct. Swamiji shows the way, through his unique ability to re-vision and re-interpret India's ancient wisdom for the modern seeker.

I trust the following pages of the book will inspire the readers to pursue the path of excellence – *yoga karmasu kausalam* – soar the sky and touch new heights in whatever endeavor he or she undertakes.

A Word Before you Read

Swami Bodhananda

The following articles were originally given as lectures to different audiences in Delhi and Chandigarh. What inspired me in formulating my thoughts in these lectures is my dream of creating an Indian style of management with ideas drawn from Indian wisdom traditions and interpreted for the needs of modern managers. I welcome and expect critical comments from practicing Indian managers and management scholars in response to the ideas expressed in this book.

The ideas highlighted in these lectures are the following:

1. India has a great future. Indian economy will grow to become the largest in the world by 2050, with a GDP of $48 trillion, surpassing the USA and China. Indian work force will dominate an aging world economy by 2035.
2. India must whole-heartedly embrace globalization and the capitalist market economy.
3. Competition is the law of nature. No society can ignore its operations in resource allocation among individuals, classes and nations.
4. Indian wisdom tradition and mythology are rich with insights applicable to modern management problems.
5. Individual consciousness is the key resource in economic development and evolutionary progress.
6. Consciousness is infinite potentiality, which can be transformed into health, energy and happiness in individual lives and ideas, concepts, designs and products in the interactive world.
7. No human decision can be perfect. Leadership is the art of creating optimal solutions.

8. There are four types of leadership: manipulative, transactional, transformational and transcendental. The best among them is the self-giving transcendental leadership.
9. There are four types of energy namely negergy, energy, synergy and hynergy. Smart organizations avoid negergy producing relationships and organizational structures and aspire to create synergy producing group dynamics leading to hynergies.
10. There are four ways of conflict resolution such as, *sama* – collaboration, *dana* – conciliation, *bheda* – disruption, and *danda* – use of force. A wise leader resorts to all these methods depending on the situation and the stratagems of the adversary.
11. There are four human goals. They are *dharma* – balanced power, *artha* – wealth, *kama* – pleasures, and *moksha* – freedom. A wise person pursues these goals in a judicious manner to maximize his growth and fulfillment.

The overriding thesis that I present here is that humans are essentially spiritual and a field of infinite potentialities, which is to be explored and expressed through self-giving productive work in an interactive world.

INDIAN ETHOS

1

Spirituality in the Workplace*

Mind poised in balance, ready to take pleasure and pain, gain and loss, victory and defeat in your stride, prepare yourself then for battle; you will not thus incur sin.

Bhagavad Gita: 2:38

Spirituality and Wealth Creation

As management practitioners, your job is to create wealth by putting scarce resources to optimal use and by creating value for the customer's money. That is how modern management is defined. If you do not do that, then you have no business to be in business. You cannot escape that duty in the name of spirituality. If you are in business investing your hard-earned money you have to be competitive, productive and ensure a net profit. If you don't do that, I have no sympathy for you. The question is how do you achieve this task? How do you create value for the customer's money and how can spirituality help you in that enterprise? How can the science of mind or the

---

*Lecture delivered at All India Management Association (AIMA) New Delhi on 21st March 2003

Indian wisdom tradition help you in this project? I would like to tailor my talk around this question- *how can spirituality contribute to the creation of a pool of globally competent and effective managers?*

We all know that the world is shrinking and as they say, we are celebrating life in a global village. The world is constantly pouring into our drawing rooms. We cannot ignore what is happening in Vietnam, or in Chechnya, or in Kashmir, or what is happening in the forums of the WTO and UN, or who is benefiting by the globalization process or what happens to the neglected and marginalized people and their lives and livelihood. We also cannot ignore what is happening to our environment, what is happening to native cultures, and what will happen to us when we become a global monoculture. If everybody is eating the same kind of food, dressing the same way, speaking the same language, using the same consumer goods, what will happen to the cultural diversity that is the basis of our survival? These issues illustrate the need for the modern management world to incorporate spiritual and ethical values.

How do we approach the issue of ethics and spirituality in the process of wealth creation? Can spirituality create effective managers who are ethically sound and pragmatically creative? The West is seeking this kind of knowledge from India. There are a lot of management gurus in the West who are borrowing from the Indian wisdom tradition. They take an idea, develop it, make it workable, clothe it in simple language and sell it. They are very clever at marketing ideas. We have a treasure-chest of management ideas in the Bhagavad Gita, the Upanishads, Mahabharata, the Panchatantra and the Arthashastra. Great wisdom is locked up in those texts, but alas, we do not know how to unlock them, how to interpret them, how to apply them in facing modern challenges. Of late we have failed in knowledge creation.

Some people ask, 'How has India become so backward? India has such a wonderful wisdom tradition, a colorful history and had a rich and thriving civilization. What happened?' Generally the answer given is that we lagged behind in technology, science and in modern management practices. We have the wisdom, we are proud of it, we can speak about it, but we do not know how to apply it. We can talk about excellence for two hours but we cannot make a good pair of shoes, a good knife or a good transistor. The wisdom is there, but we are not able to put it into practice. We talk about *satyam*, we talk about *ahimsa*, but when it comes to practice, we fail. What I see in the Indian situation is that we are unable to put our knowledge into practical use. There seems to exist some disconnect between knowing and doing.

Developing Values

I feel that in order to understand the role of spirituality in the world of business our values have to be understood and interpreted in relation to the activity of wealth creation. You cannot practice values in the Himalayas. Honesty, non-violence, love, sharing, hard work, all these values cannot be practiced sitting in isolation. Somebody said, 'I was twenty years in the Himalayan caves and I was practicing truthfulness.' He could do so because for twenty years he never met anybody there, he never borrowed money from anybody. It is easy to practice truth, non-violence, tolerance or the value of sharing in the caves of the Himalayas. Most of the intellectuals for the last two thousand years in India have been following this illusion, going to the mountains, sitting there and contemplating. A stage comes when their brains do not function simply because they are not challenged.

The brain has to be challenged continuously. The challenge comes from outside. The sensations have to constantly stimulate you, so that the mind becomes active and brings out the Spirit. Otherwise the Spirit remains un-manifested. The Spirit manifests through the instrumentality of the mind engaged in work. We have to break out of our insipid ways of thinking and follow the teachings of the Bhagavad Gita. The challenge is how to practice these values in the midst of our daily lives, in the family, in the community, in the market place, across the table in business transactions. It is very easy to talk about these values in the air, but it is very difficult to practice them on the solid ground of our daily life. That is why, when Arjuna wanted to go to the Himalayas and practice meditation and spiritual values, Krishna told him, 'You will have to practice spirituality in the midst of the battle field.' The challenge before us is how to practice these values while we are engaged in the world, in our wealth creating activities. That challenge needs to be addressed by the Indian people and the Indian management theoreticians.

Spirituality has to be expressed in action

We want to sit in the Security Council, we want to be one of the major super powers, we want to influence the world policies – we have all these ambitions. But what do we do about it? How are we preparing our people, our students, our teachers, our leaders and our managers for this task? That is the most important question we have to face today. People say that Indians are basically and traditionally spiritual. What exactly is this spirituality? Is spirituality something different from your daily life? I would not call it spirituality, if alienated from daily life. You cannot have a double life. Here in the corporate world you often follow all kinds of unethical policies and practices. On the weekend you go to Tirupati and offer some money to the Lord and request the Lord to wash off all your sins. That kind of spirituality has no meaning at all. *If you want to really understand spirituality, it has to be practiced in your daily life. This is the core teaching of the Indian wisdom tradition.*

In the Indian tradition the whole world is an extension of the Spirit, whereas in the Western tradition the world is seen as something different from God. According to the West, after creating the world God chose to sit in heaven above his creation. However, in our wisdom tradition, God – the Spirit lives in the heart of every single individual. When we say spirituality, we mean activating that Spirit latent in our hearts. Even though it is invisible, the Spirit is your inherent, inexhaustible and innate potentiality. We just have to make it patent; we have to bring it out while we interact with the world. So, how do we bring that potentiality about while we are interacting with the world?

The Bhagavad Gita, the quintessence of Indian wisdom tradition, gives us the answer. Arjuna was confused about what to do in the battlefield of Kurukshetra. Krishna shared his wisdom. And at the end of the teaching, Arjuna says, 'I am ready for action'. Therefore, *spirituality has to express itself in action.*

You may be meditating everyday, you may be chanting all the mantras, you may be visiting temples, but if you don't bring it into action, if you cannot put it into moment-to-moment responses to the challenging situations of the world, you cannot say you are practicing spirituality. If this active expression of the Spirit is how we understand spirituality, then how do we go about realizing it?

The Spirit Has To Be Activated

In the Bhagavad Gita, Arjuna represents action and Krishna contemplative consciousness. According to the Gita, when these two factors join there is *shree* (wealth), *vijaya* (success), *bhuti* (prosperity), and *niti* (justice) (Bhagavad Gita, 18.78). How we combine contemplation with action and realize these values is the management question. First of all, we have to understand that as human beings we are not just the physical body. We have a mind and behind the mind is the invisible Spirit, which is connected to our consciousness.

Consciousness is coming in a big way into the modern discourse, especially in the management and even in the scientific world. What is consciousness? This is a subject that the Indian wisdom tradition is well versed in. We are basically conscious people. Through contemplation, meditation and good work, we can touch the level of consciousness. Consciousness is a field of infinite potentiality. It is our very Spirit. It is not physical potential that we are talking about. Physically you may be weak. The man on the street may be stronger than you. And it is not your mental or intellectual strength that is important because another person may be more intelligent than you. What is your real strength? It is your spiritual strength. You need to learn how to be spiritually strong like Mahatma Gandhi. It was said that the Spirit was aflame in him. He was in constant communication with the Spirit. Then only you can develop real strength. Then only you can tackle life's problems effectively.

The Spirit has to be activated, manifested. It is the Spirit that brings life and vibrancy into the world. If you don't activate the Spirit you feel repressed, you feel limited, you feel unhappy and you feel frustrated. The reason for your frustration is not that you have not achieved anything in the world materially, but that you have not touched the Spirit in you. Your potential remains unexplored. It is something like a person who is a good singer who has got a lot of music in his heart and wants to share it with the world but does not create the opportunity to sing. You feel repressed and frustrated when your heart doesn't find expression. One reason for mental illnesses and psychological dysfunctions is that we are not touching the Spirit latent in us. Most of us don't even know there is a spiritual dimension in us. Let alone how to tap into it. You have to know, explore and express those spiritual potentialities.

For example, if you simply sit down you cannot develop your muscles. You have potential muscles within you but you cannot develop them unless you regularly lift weights. If you want to learn swimming you have to jump into the ocean. This is how you activate the Spirit. Unless you explore you cannot discover your potential. There is the spiritual potential in you, but it has to be manifested, and for that you have to interact with the world. We will discuss three main skills you need to develop in order to effectively manifest your spiritual power in your work and in your life.

Pursue Excellence in Work

The Gita says you can never avoid work. But in practice we spend our whole life trying to avoid work. Whether you are in the government, in a private office or at home, you use all your smartness to avoid work. Gita's dictum is that no human being can ever avoid work. If you do not work, then some work will be forced upon you. Even if you are an old man of 90 years you cannot avoid work. If you give up work you lose your dignity and self-respect. Without work you are not challenged. You are a dead person without work.

So the only question that remains is, with what attitude and with what expectation should you engage in work? The Bhagavad Gita says, 'Spirituality means pursuit of excellence in work. Work has to be a means of pursuing excellence, for excellence is God,' (2.50). This is the first attitude required to manifest your potentiality. Spirituality is excellence in work, excellence is God, and excellence has no limit. You can go on and on in the pursuit of excellence, because excellence is an infinite value. There is no end to self-expansion. Whatever you do, put your heart and soul into it. Bring a good product out of it. Pick up a rusted piece of iron, put it in the fire, and when it is red-hot, hammer it and make a good knife that has exchange value. This act of creation brings the best out of you. It is an expression of your inner sense of worth and wellness. I would call this experience spirituality.

Why in India did we lose this great message of the Gita? Our idea of spirituality is someone sitting in a corner chanting Ram, Ram, Ram. I heard a funny story about a devotee who was always chanting Ram. When the devotee died, Yama, the Lord of Death, thought that he must be sent to Vaikunta, the abode of Rama. Yama enquired from managers running Vaikunta, 'Should I send him there?' It seems Rama told Yama, he did not want the devotee to come because he would not give Rama any peace of mind, all the time sitting around saying Ram, Ram, Ram, disturbing Rama in his work. The moral of the story is that God loves those who are engaged in work, performing their duties and sharing the burden of the world with Him. That is the first definition of spirituality. A spiritual person is one who is excellent in the work place, in his home and in all his relationships.

You have to have a very dynamic spirituality, a spirituality in which your intellect is encouraged to take risks and where your energies are put into inspiring projects. Most spiritual people avoid risks. Not knowing that by taking risks we give ourselves the opportunity to expand. The very law of life is expansion. If a company does not grow, it will die. If your company does not expand, it will contract and disappear. How you expand is up to you. Movement is the insignia of life. You cannot avoid it.

Self-confidence is an important skill you must develop when facing risky situations. You have to create self-confidence in order to tap into the infinite consciousness and bring out your full potential. Conversely, self-confidence gets boosted when you realize your potential. They are mutually reinforcing. When you are challenged you must have self-confidence to deal with the situation. When Arjuna said, 'I want to run away from this battle,' Krishna said, 'You have to stay back, fight and solve this problem.' India has enumerable problems. Does it not? There is the problem of poverty, the problem of lack of infrastructure, the problem in Kashmir, the problem of not having an Indian style of management and many such problems. As managers, you cannot avoid all these issues. If you want to become a major power you have to stand up and face these challenges. You have to take risks. You cannot, like an ostrich, just bury your head in the sand.

Control Your Reactions

As we have already said, the first definition of spirituality is the pursuit of excellence in work. But what you will find is that when you pursue excellence, many problems arise. If you don't work, there is no problem. If you don't take up challenges, there is no problem. People forget you and you forget the people. But when you start working and taking on challenges, then you experience mental disturbances, anxiety and tension. You do not know what is there in the future for you. Thus tension is a necessary concomitant of activity. You cannot avoid it. Bhagavad Gita gives a solution for this problem. The Gita advocates restraint over reaction to the fruits of your work. Work, of course, creates results. We are all anxious about the results and because of this we experience tension and anxiety.

What is meant by reaction? There are two types of reactions. The first is a reaction to an anticipated outcome. Suppose you have written an exam. You become naturally worried about the results. There is anxiety. You are reacting to an anticipated situation. You lose sleep, you have no appetite and you are angry and irritable. Then when the results come you see that you have excelled. Now you are very happy. You invite everybody for a celebration. This is the second type of reaction, the reaction to an actual outcome. When success comes you are happy, when failure comes you are unhappy. These reactions to anticipated events and actual experiences are the cause of all our stress. Krishna says, 'Having done your work to the best of your ability, leave the rest to God.' Let the universal intelligence decide how hard you worked and what reward you deserve. Do your best and leave the rest.

The modern management science has taken up this idea of non-reaction very actively. This idea is at the heart of what they call emotional intelligence. Emotional intelligence is the ability to restrain reaction and properly respond to situations. You consciously choose your responses to the dynamically changing situations around you. When you are very angry, control your anger response. I always tell this story. A person was very angry with his son and screamed at him, 'You are a son of a donkey!' Then afterwards he repented, 'Why did I say that?' But his son was quick to respond, 'Daddy, don't feel bad. It is the only truth that you have said.' Now you are a prisoner of your uncontrolled behavior! This kind of a violent unconscious response is a reaction. You must create some space inside, so that you have room to consciously design your responses to the situations. The Bhagavad Gita gives you many techniques to restrain reactions so that you can pull out appropriate responses to situations. This is the second advice that Bhagavad Gita gives.

Be Rooted in Yourself

The third advice Gita gives is that while you are doing all this you must be rooted in yourself. How do you become rooted in yourself? You should have the understanding that your happiness is within you and that nobody else can make you happy or unhappy. If somebody seems to make you unhappy, that is because you have given yourself to his manipulative tactics. If you can understand that your happiness is within you, then you see that you have a choice to be happy. Actually, happiness is an intrinsic quality of the Spirit. True happiness is not something that you feel for sometime and then it goes away. True happiness is something that you are. That is how you become a spiritually rooted person, by knowing that your very nature is happiness. Therefore, I would say a spiritually rooted person is one who is always happy. Happiness is being comfortable with oneself. When you are happy, you smile. When you smile you use only three facial muscles. When you frown, 67 muscles are used. That should tell you, it is more natural to smile than frown. When you smile, you become relaxed. You invoke your Spirit, your energy is manifested, you are able to keep control over your reactions and then you are able to pursue excellence in work.

Harness the Three Skills

You need to bring these three skills into your life.

- First, the pursuit of excellence in work;
- Second, the restraining of the mental reactions; and
- Third, rooting in the Self.

If you can harness all these three skills in your daily life you will be able to design the best and perfect responses to situations, develop an abiding state of happiness, and become a very competent manager. Modern management is essentially people-centered and culture-specific. People are the critical asset in modern management. Capital, raw material and technology are not as important as people. How people are motivated and with what zest they engage in their work are of immense value to the success of an organization.

Indian spirituality is a very important source of information for modern management. When we are poised on the 21st century, when we are trying to discover our legitimate place in the comity of nations, we must have our own management style, something which is different from the Western, European or Japanese style. Our management insight is to create managers who are *sthitaprajnas*. That is the word used in the Bhagavad Gita. *Sthitaprajna* is a person of steady wisdom or self-knowledge who can never be shaken. Such enlightened people are not dictated by their circumstances in choosing their responses. We have the wisdom tradition, we have the vocabulary and we have the insight. What is necessary is to interpret our scriptures, process that information, create knowledge, and then pass it on to practicing managers so that they can apply it in day-to-day situations.

My advice to you managers is to go back to the Indian wisdom tradition with a critical mind. Do not follow blindly all that is said there. That is another danger I see these days. Whenever some discovery comes from the West, we say that it was first discovered in India. When the West invented the flying machine, immediately we said, 'Oh! Sri Rama also flew in an aircraft.'

But then I ask you, 'Sir, can somebody read that book and manufacture an aircraft?' The answer will be a resounding no. Then what is the use of such empty claims! Therefore, our wisdom tradition has to be seen with a critical eye. Does it help us? You must critically investigate. I do not subscribe to the theme that everything past in India is good. There is a lot which has to be ignored in the Indian wisdom tradition. With that in mind, we will have to go into the wisdom tradition and then bring out what is relevant for the modern world and modern management and I am sure we will benefit immensely from that exercise.

2

Personality Re-engineering*

Beyond the waking, dream and sleep states; beyond the conscious, unconscious and memories; beyond ignorance, knowledge and intuition; beyond all thoughts, feeling and psychic modifications; beyond all qualities, definitions and words; beyond sights and forms; revealed in the silence of the pure heart I exist. In me, worlds and words resolve. I am peace absolute, goodness absolute and oneness absolute. I am the fourth dimension, the great beyond and I am Siva.

Mandukya Upanishad: Mantra 7

We are living in a wonderful time. They say India is shining and that all Indians are experiencing the feel-good factor. Though I have my own reservations, I am happy to share that feeling and the kind of euphoria being generated in our country. I have heard that if you fake it, you can make it. If we can truly create the feeling that India can make it, India will make it. That is the faith that I have and I invite you to join me and hold that faith aloft.

Our President, respected A.P.J. Abdul Kalam, has said that India will become a middle-income economy by 2020. I think that is a great, realizable dream that the President has for us. India has the potential. If Malaysia and South Korea can become

*Lecture delivered at All India Management Association (AIMA), New Delhi on 10th March 2004.

a middle-income economy in 20 years, I see no reason why India, with the sound economic base that we have now, should not also become a middle-income economy. If we want to inspire our people we have to give them tangible and quantitative goals. If we simply say that India should grow, that is not enough for the people. They need a vision that is measurable. It is only if we can hold that vision that we will be able to inspire our people, our managers, our leaders, our scientists, our students to organize themselves and realize this goal.

Let me repeat, our goal for India is to become a middle-income economy by 2020, which means that our annual per capita income must grow to the tune of $12,000 to bring us even with Malaysia and South Korea. Then alone India can be considered a middle-income economy. At present, India's per capita income is a meager $500. So from $500 within a period of 20 years, our per capita income should grow to $12,000. In terms of rupees this means that from the present Rupees 25,000 our per capita income should grow to Rupees 500,000 annually. Can we do it? That is a big question. But we should do it. Then alone we can fulfill our vision of becoming a super power, an independent center of civilization, creating values and knowledge with a sense of pride and having the freedom to participate in the global economy.

Samuel Huntington, the Harvard historian, has said that India is one of the countries that will quickly rise and become a major contributor to the world economic process. He says India, China, United Europe and the United States of America, these four conglomerates or nations will play a vital role in forming the world order in the 21st century. Are we Indians conscious of our own destiny? Are we feeling that kind of a pride within ourselves? India can become a creative and influential player in the world order and world economics. India can become a superpower at par with the United States, United Europe and China. If this is understood as our goal to be realized in concrete terms, the question arises, who will lead us to that destiny? Do we have the managerial and political leadership to achieve this ambitious goal within the short time period of 20 years?

If we are going to lift India from its present position to the highest position that we aspire to, we have to change our mindset. That is what we are discussing this evening. And what kind of change needs to take place? Quite simply, the change that we have to create is the shift from an attitude of *we can't* to an attitude of *we can*. If Malaysia can do it, if Singapore can do it, if Taiwan can do it, if South Korea can do it, India can also do it. And to become prosperous is not against the Asian value system. I have heard people say that India is a spiritual country and that India is not interested in material development, or that India is other-worldly, that India is comfortable living in dirt and poverty because Indians think that the world is *mithya* or *maya* or illusion. That is the kind of canard or false idea that the West has spread about India. We must remember that India was at one time a very prosperous civilization. Somewhere down the road India lost it, and now the time has come to recapture the glory that we once enjoyed

How do we change the mindset of our political leaders? Mr. Atal Bihari Vajpeyi, the Indian Prime Minister goes to America and nobody notices him. It is very painful. A leader of a one-thousand-million-strong Nation that aspires to be a super power in 20 years blatantly ignored! In America and Europe nobody bothers about Indian Prime Ministers, and no newspaper reports their visits. When the Chinese President visits France he is given a grand welcome. The longest red carpet you can imagine is spread from the airport to the presidential palace. When he goes to America the President invites him to his summer camp and secret discussions take place between them. But when the Indian Prime Minister visits the United States, he has to stay in a nearby hotel and he does not get any invitations to private meetings with the President. Why should such things happen? Why don't we carry respect in other countries? We say 30,000 Indians are doctors in America, so many Microsoft employees are Indians, 30 percent of NASA employees are Indians and so on and so forth. But still our voice is not heard in the foreign countries. Why? We have to think about this problem and develop the required mindset. Presently, India does not have that fire in the belly, as they say.

Let us plant these quantifiable dreams in our mind. India has to be a super power. India has to sit in the Security Council. India must have hydrogen bombs. India must have intercontinental ballistic missiles. India must send a man to the moon. Not for any other purpose but to create confidence, to uplift the morale of the people. It is something like in the olden days when people used to conduct *Ashvamedha* and *Vajapeya yajnas*. What was the purpose? It was to bring the people together, to brainstorm, to work together, to think big and dream big. Just to create a culture of thinking big these *yajnas* were performed. We have to re-invent that kind of culture. We have to think big and we have to achieve bigger and bigger things.

That is the change of mindset that is necessary. How do we do that? Where do we begin?

The modern economic and management theories say that the individual is the most important factor in economic development. It is not technology or organizational principles alone that matter. The Indian wisdom tradition says that the individual is the ultimate resource and that if you can change the individual you can change organizations. What do we mean by that? This is the theme of today's talk: how to re-engineer the personality and re-invent the individual.

What is the Indian concept of personality? The West has the psychological theories of Sigmund Freud, David Hume, Adler, Abraham Maslow or Pavlov who expound the western concept of personality. These theories are based on the binary thinking traditions of the Judeo-Christians, Greco-Romans and Anglo-Saxons. We, in India too, have a concept of the individual. In fact, our tradition has spent considerable time and effort delving into the complexities of the human personality and has developed effective methods of understanding and utilizing our unique potential as human beings. What is or who is the human being? What are his talents? How does he fit into the world around him? How can he manifest his latent strength and wisdom? In the modern world where the individual is the center of economic activities and is the critical economic resource, we must draw from the Indian wisdom tradition to help us realize the full potential of the individual.

This concept of personality re-engineering is borrowed from the Western management jargon. Unfortunately, unless confirmed by the West, we will not take any idea seriously. That is why I coined the term 'personality re-engineering.' It is a concept borrowed from the book 'Re-engineering the Corporation,' by Michael Hammer and James Champy. In that book they talk about re-engineering business processes. They say that a corporation has to become flexible, lean, mean and flat and that all unnecessary organizational structures have to be demolished. They further contend that all members of the organization have to know all functions in the organization and have to participate in the creation of visions and values for the organization. It has to be a bottom-up, not top-down organization. The corporation should become an organism, not a mechanism, and it should flow like a river. In an organism each organ is partially independent, but it cooperates with all the other systems in the maintenance of the organism. So he talks about such an organization that is very dynamic, flexible and devoid of unnecessary bureaucratic structures.

This is a good theory for business re-engineering, but the Indian wisdom tradition says that you cannot reorganize an organization unless you first reorganize the individuals in the organization. If we can create change in the individual, the organizational re-engineering will happen automatically. So, how do we change the individuals, their mindset, without which no lasting organizational change can take place? Today we will be discussing five different aspects of personality re-engineering.

What is the Indian concept of an individual? Our self-concept is important because as we think, so we become. Our thoughts and our self-image influence our behavior and our actions in the world. If I think I am a worm, then I will act as a worm in this world. Whenever I see a bird, a crow or a peacock, I will shudder. I will run away from all these animals. If I think I am a lion, then I will roar like a lion. What you think, that you feel, and what you feel, that you act, and what you act, that you become. So our thoughts about ourselves, our self-image, is very important.

Self-image usually is a product of culture. It is your culture that decides your self-image, not you. During the British period we thought we were useless people because that is what they were telling us repeatedly. And that, somehow, got into our system, our psyche, and we lived in a kind of enslaved mentality for a while. But if we look back into our history, we see that our *rishis* had a very different vision about the individual. They used to say, '*amritasya putrah*' meaning 'children of immortality.' You are not just physical beings with facial features, with a bone structure, and blood and marrow. Beneath the physical body you have a very powerful mind, and beyond the mind you have a spiritual center. Essentially you are a spiritual person and thereafter you are a physical person. You are a spirit with a body, not a body with a spirit. That is the true Indian vision, the way we should see all human beings. I think it is time for us to recapture that vision. It is only if that vision dominates your thinking and determines your self-image that you can correctly evaluate yourself and can begin the process of personality re-engineering. So a kind of a paradigm shift has to happen for which the following five principles need to be contemplated upon:

1. Invoking the Spirit

I remember an old children's story. When Alexander came to India he wanted to meet a *rishi*. When he finally did meet one he was so much impressed with him he said, 'Please, come with me to Greece. I will give you a fabulous palace there.' The *rishi* responded, 'Didn't you come here because you were unhappy there? Why should I come with you and share your unhappiness?' Alexander was further impressed. He pleaded, 'You must come! I am so much amazed by your wisdom, your equanimity and your balance of mind. I want to take you with me.' The *rishi* protested, 'No, I cannot come. I am happy here. I do not want to come.' Alexander became angry and drew his sword. 'I demand that you come,' he said. 'If you don't then you will suffer dearly.' The *rishi* laughed at Alexander and said, 'What can you do with this sword? You may cut my body, but my body is already perishing. My spirit is immortal, and you cannot do anything to that.' Alexander was even more impressed. Even when he drew his sword to kill him, the *rishi* remained *akshobhya* – undisturbed. The calm equanimity of the *rishi* mesmerized Alexander, and his anger quickly disappeared. Finally he said, 'I am very happy now. I want to give you a gift. Ask me something and please bless me.' The *rishi* said, 'Please do this, you move away from the path of the sun. I am feeling a little cold.'

This is the kind of courage and depth of vision that we had once upon a time. We have to regain that wisdom. We are not just this body. There is a spiritual dimension in us. On some level we are all aware of this Spirit. Don't we say that you must be a 'spirited' manager? We should show spirited enthusiasm and energy in the work place? So the Spirit is the keyword in the modern management world. How do you become a spirited manager? Not by drinking liquor. That is not the kind of spirit we are talking about. We are talking about the Spirit that you draw from within. Developing that kind of faith in oneself is very important. The Spirit can be invoked through contemplation, inner calm and other creative processes. And, the same Spirit can be morphed into products. That is the great idea that the *rishis* talk about. It is not that the Spirit is contacted by meditation and then forgotten about. Once the Spirit is invoked through meditation it should be converted into thoughts, ideas, processes and innovative products. The word 'product' is an inclusive term which means, 'any tangible or intangible value, which can give satisfaction to human beings and help them grow.' It can be anything from a smile to a consoling word, a service to a consumable good. I can pick up a piece of leather and meditate on that and invoke my Spirit and come out with a pair of shoes for human use. So Spirit should be manifested and transformed into material, tangible products. That is how the *rishi* understood the Spirit.

This vision of oneself, that you are basically the Spirit, has to be propagated. Fortunately, the modern world is grudgingly moving towards this idea. Haven't you heard about the concept of body, mind and Spirit? In the medical circle, management circle, in the legal circle, everywhere they talk about the Spirit. The Spirit, though, is invisible. You cannot see it with your eyes. But the Spirit can be experienced in terms of health, intelligence and energy. The Indian wisdom tradition teaches us that every human being has this hidden reservoir of energy that can be invoked for creative activity. It is not that when you meet the Spirit you dissolve away. That is not what we are talking about. We are talking about a Spirit that can be contacted, invoked and translated into daily living.

A creative and fulfilling life is possible by living in effortless contact with the Spirit. When you disconnect from the Spirit you develop all kinds of problems. That is why medical doctors these days ask you to meditate for healing purposes. Ninety percent of our medical problems are because we wrongly believe we are sick. Actually, in a way, we never really become sick. Sickness is a thought. It is the product of a false belief system, a belief system that is not rooted in the Spirit. Modern medical science has been successful in convincing you that you can fall sick so that they can treat you. You don't have to believe that. Even if your doctors say you are sick, let them worry about that. That's their problem.

The Eastern wisdom tradition talks about spiritual healing. Modern quantum physics also hints about the possibility of such healing. Quantum physics deconstructs everything to a position where there are only potentialities and a range of possibilities. They call this the 'quantum soup.' Modern physics is increasingly coming to the conclusion that this field of possibilities could be consciousness itself, a position that the Vedantins of the Indian wisdom tradition have held for thousands of years. The physicists say that there seems to be a quantum leap from consciousness to matter. With this new perspective, scientists are saying that everything, the stars and planets, mountains and rivers, animals and trees, and the entire panorama of creation emerges from this quantum soup via subatomic particles like protons, neutrons and electrons. It is these same particles that form the molecules that make up everything in the world around us.

Human biology tells us that a human being begins its life as a single cell of 46 chromosomes gathered from the father and mother. And that single cell divides into 135 stem cells, and from these 135 cells this bag of billions upon billions of cells that we call an Einstein or a Mahatma Gandhi is miraculously created. All of us are born from that single cell. So that one single cell has the potential to create trillions and trillions of cells, specialized tissues and organs, and finally the cultured human being. From one single seed emerges a huge tree.

From this we can understand that we are fields of infinite potentiality. We are pure consciousness. That is what the Indian *rishis* meant by the mantra *'shivoham,'* (I am Shiva). When you go to an Indian guru to talk about your problems, whether you are a manager, or a doctor or a lawyer, they give one single piece of advice. And that advice is to chant *shivoham* mantra. We feel confused because we don't have that inner rooting. We have lost the inner center. Our center is outside of us and because of this we are floating like a piece of cotton in the storm. We have no anchoring at all. We have no roots. We have lost our footing. So, most people are thoroughly confused.

When you go to a guru, he will listen to you like any psychologist. The psychologist sits at your head and asks you to tell him about your problems. You tell him all of your troubles. You talk about your problems at work, with your wife, with your children, everything that is bothering you, and what does he do? He dozes off. After your one-hour monologue the session is over and you shell out five hundred rupees and go home.

Similarly, the guru listens to you and at the end asks you to chant this mantra, *shivoham,* 'You are Auspiciousness.' When the guru says, you are Shiva it does not mean you have to dress up like Shiva with snakes around your neck and *ashes* on your forehead and tiger skin around your waist. That is not the idea. 'You are Shiva' means that you are pure consciousness, a field of infinite potentialities. Shiva sits in meditation and then he emerges into his cosmic dance. The whole universe becomes manifest as Shiva dances. When he meditates the whole universe collapses into him. So, Shiva has the power to create, to sustain and to destroy. So do you. Such is the power that modern managers need. They need the power to create, the power to sustain, and when the life of that creation is over, they also need the detached power to destroy their own creation. Modern management talks about creative destruction.

One has to constantly meditate on one's true nature, as *shivoham*. This is the mantra the Indian manager should recite every day, if he wants to capture his own inner potential, his only valuable resource. Then alone he can be a creative agent of change in the modern world. You need not be ashamed of chanting this mantra. You say, 'How can I do that? I am a manager, a secularist and a rational thinker. I believe in analytical thinking.' But you forget that *shivoham* is your fundamental truth. You are only asserting and announcing your true nature. I can assure you that if you managers chant *shivoham* everyday for half an hour, you can become the top-notch managers and the top-notch leaders in the world. If you really don't like that word use modern scientific jargons like, 'I am a field of infinite potentiality,' or, 'Day by day, every day, I am growing.' Keep on repeating it and what you say daily, that you will eventually become. You can say, 'I am Shiva,' or you can say 'I am *shava,*' 'I am life,' or 'I am death.' The choice is yours. You can condemn yourself by saying, 'I am only an instrument in the hands of others,' or you can assert yourself and transform yourself by saying, 'I am an independent agent of value creation.' You have the choice to be a dependent thing or an autonomous person. You are a field of infinite power. Instead of doubting me, sitting there like a question mark and challenging me, believe in what I say. Chant the mantra and see the results. The test of the pudding is in its eating. See how it transforms your thought processes, how it makes you a courageous risk-taking individual and an effective group leader. This is the first requirement of personality re-engineering: developing an abiding faith in ones own infinitude.

2. Personality Grows from Inside Out

The second requirement of personality re-engineering or personality development is to recognize that the personality grows from within, inside out. The general idea of personality growth is that it happens from outside in by changing our external appearance. With that idea you change your hairstyle or change your style of dress or you change your style of speaking. You start developing a western look, speak in crisp London English, or change the décor of your office. Then you think you are a modern manager. That is your idea of personality change. The modern world thinks that by painting the outside you will create a good impression. You use nice words that don't reflect your thoughts, creating inner conflict and dissipating your personality. External change without internal change is meaningless. Actually, personality development must start with your self-image.

Let us think of our personality development as growing from the inside out like a seed that grows into a tree. Whatever is latent in the seed that alone can become the tree! This is a radically different concept from the modern concept of personality development. What you think determines your words, your words determine your deeds, your deeds determine your habits, your habits determine your character and your character creates your destiny. Your destiny begins from that little seed of intention that becomes the huge tree of your personality. All of that begins from the little seed of intention. Unless we change our attitude, the change that we aspire for in the world is not possible.

So what should our intention be? Presently our intention in any activity is to gather, to draw everything towards us. This is because we think that we have to develop ourselves from the outside in and we think that happiness comes from the outside. But now we see that this is not true. Now we see that our potentiality springs from within and expresses itself out into the world. Once you have this kind of self-image, from there comes the right kind of intention. You discover that your intention should be one of giving and sharing and helping others to grow. You understand that the more you give, the more you will be given. The fact of the matter is that this economics of gaining by giving has been forgotten. This is largely due to the fact that we are still operating in a field of limitless needs and limited resources. Economics is the study of human behavior trying to meet limitless needs with limited resources. Economics is a science of choices, of how human beings make choices. In a situation where needs are limitless and resources are scarce we generally don't think about giving unless we get first. But spiritual economics warns us, 'You will get only what you give. Whatever you give will come back to you. Whatever you gather, whatever you snatch from others, will perish in your hands.' So from a change of self-image arises the right intention, and from this comes the right attitude of giving and sharing, and such people will create a mutually nourishing, cherishing and growing environment. This is what we call synergy, the win-win situation.

3. Growth by Facing Challenges

The third aspect of personality re-engineering is the idea that you grow by facing challenges. Growth is determined by the way you face challenges. You will not unfold your potentiality without facing challenges. After discovering your potential you have to make it patent. Otherwise you feel bored and frustrated. You have to put your potential to use and facing challenges creatively is the way to do it. When you don't grow you are bored. Boredom makes you listless. The moment somebody starts speaking you feel sleepy. There is no mind to listen fully. This boredom or lack of interest is because we are not growing. We are not unfolding our potentiality. How do you unfold your potentiality? There is no other way of actualizing your potentiality than engaging yourself in challenging activities. If you simply sit in a cave and do nothing you will never realize your true glory.

Suppose you want to develop your bicep muscles. Everyday you have to lift weights, heavier and heavier each day, and as you progress you are able to make your hidden muscle potential manifest. You develop bulging muscles. But if you don't do that, if you think, 'How can I lift weight unless I have strength in my muscle?' you are denying the chance of developing your muscles. So in the same way, to develop your potential you have to invite challenges. You have to invite more and more challenges, more and more risk. The more the merrier. No risk, no hope for growth. So when we talk of spirituality we are not talking about withdrawal from the world. The world is there for you to realize who you are. And hence the third principle of personality growth is that one has to welcome challenges.

Now, globalization is a great challenge. Multinationals are coming with better products and cheaper prices and better service. Why are people buying Chinese products over Indian products? Quite simply, the Chinese products are bought because they are cheaper, of better quality and are easily available. Why are Indian products not seen? Not because people are not wanting them, but because we are lacking in these three aspects. The Chinese work hard and provide better service. Why is the American market flooded with Chinese goods? The reasons are the same. And people buying them are not unpatriotic. Patriotism does not mean we have to buy shoddy products. We are intelligent patriots. We should take upon ourselves these challenges of globalization. Globalization is an opportunity for us to hone our talents, to discover our potential, to express on the world stage. Greater and greater challenges have to be welcomed. Risks have to be taken. Then alone personality growth is possible.

The more challenges you face, the better you are. In the process you may perish. That is welcome. There is no point in living like a worm. The attitude should be: 'let me die like a hero, rather than live like a zero'. If you want to be a global player then you must be able to roll up your sleeves and jump into the global arena. Don't complain that you don't have a level playing field. Who is going to give you a level playing field? Who is going to provide you with such an advantage? We don't have a Karna, who was willing to give up his armor in the name of charity. Nobody is going to give you any charity. America is not going to give you a level playing field. With one hand you have to fight, and with the other you will have to level the playing field, all by yourself. Others will not allow you the leisure to catch up. Why should they? You have to do it single-handedly. These challenges have to be taken up boldly in order to succeed in the global arena and to discover your own innate potential.

4. Detached Engagement

Now let us explore the fourth principle: detached engagement. I hear a lot of people talking about competition in a derogatory manner these days. They say that because of competition people are losing their jobs. I believe that this is true. If you don't have the fire inside you, competition can finish you off, it can make you sick. But if you have the fire in you, competition can help you grow. The competitive world is necessary to challenge and invoke the human Spirit. We have to accept it. But at the same time, when we engage in the competitive world we have to do so in a way that people and industries don't become sick due to all the stress and strain. The issue is how do we engage in the competitive world and become a creative player while at the same time keeping our health, sanity and balance? That is a big challenge.

The Indian wisdom tradition says that you have to engage in the world with a detached mind. Detached engagement is the mantra. If you simply detach, you will be worthless to the world. You will become lazy and waste your time in fruitless criticism. So simple detachment is dangerous because you aren't engaged in life, you aren't facing your challenges. But simple engagement is also dangerous because you become overwhelmed by the challenges you face. You are stressed and exhausted. You feel anxious. Your mind is not prepared to face the challenges. So what is necessary is detached engagement.

I was recently reading the biography of Dhirubhai Ambani. At the age of 54 he had a stroke. This would not have happened if he had the mindset of detached engagement. He was a highly creative person who changed the industrial culture in our country and his contribution was very valuable. But because he did not know how to manage his challenges in a detached manner he suffered dearly. This is an important teaching of Indian wisdom tradition. You can be a great worker and a great achiever without compromising your health. Your productivity can be maintained along with your productive capacity. P and PC both can be maintained, provided we have the attitude of detachment. A little bit of prayer in the morning, a little bit of meditation, and a little bit of understanding about this complex and changing world that things are not under your control will help you a great deal. So that kind of comfort level has to be cultivated.

5. Follow Your Bliss

The final principle of personality re-engineering is the principle: 'Follow your bliss.' At the end of Bhagavad Gita, Krishna told

Arjuna, 'Whatever I have said, think about it, but do as you please. Make your own choice. Follow your bliss.' There is some internal mechanism in you, say the conscience, which tells you constantly how you have to act. That is the purpose of spiritual education: to awaken this conscience, the inner light, the inner voice and the path of bliss. If that inner force is not awakened then you are just a machine, operated by external forces, a salivating Pavlovian dog. You may be successful, but as Christ said, 'Of what avail is the whole world at the cost of the soul?' So this ability to understand and follow your bliss and act courageously and freely has to be cultivated.

When all these five principles are followed you achieve real personality re-engineering. You become a very dynamic person. When challenges come your way, you are able to spontaneously respond without any reaction. You expand your horizons at every turn. Follow these five principles and discover your inner potentiality.

3

Guna Analysis – Understanding the Human Mind*

The objective world made up of energies of reflectivity, activity and stability and constituted of mind and matter exist for the enjoyment and self-realization of the conscious individual.

Patanjali Yogasutra: 2:18

Management deals with people. Management is culture specific and people centered. To succeed in the business world we have to motivate people as workers, as consumers and as shareholders. We must have a way of helping people to bring out their best in the work place and create optimal value for the customer's money. It is in this context that we are trying to understand the human mind. Apart from understanding the world with which we interact, we also have to understand the human mind, the human Spirit and the human personality. How does the human mind behave and how does the individual make choices?

There are many different theories that the business leaders of today are drawing from in their attempt to optimize the

*Lecture delivered to MBA students at IIT Delhi on 4th April 2004.

productivity of the workforce and to please the minds of their customers. Management borrows heavily from psychology, sociology, economics, and other sciences. Freud talks about the unconscious mind and how the unconscious determines human behaviour. Economists talk about rational choices and how human beings try to maximize their advantages in a given situation by making rational choices. Sociologists talk about the need for collective survival. There are theories that talk about the drive for power. People make efforts to belong to a group and then dominate it and then through their group dominate other groups. This is the conditioned behaviour psychologists talk about. We are programmed animals. The external environment controls most public and private behaviour. Human beings behave in a deterministic manner in any given situation. If I give you a product at a higher cost and another at a lower cost then which one will you choose? Of course, you will choose the product that costs you less. Then comes the consideration of quality. You may be willing to pay a higher price for a quality product. Thus behaviour is determined by a combination of external factors and it becomes predictable. This is known as Pavlovian human behavior. Now let us see what our own wisdom tradition has to say about the psychology of human behavior.

The Theory of the *Gunas*

Is there anything we could call Indian psychology? Is there an established theory of how the average Indian behaves? Not only is there an established theory, but also it is the ideal theory for us as Indians. We should try to understand the Indian worldview using our own wisdom of the human mind so that you as managers and leaders of the future can have a grip over the Indian psyche and mindset. That is what motivated me to give you a talk on the *guna* theory.

Basis of the *Gunas* – *Purusha* and *Prakriti*

Before we discuss the *guna* theory and how it can be applied to the workplace, we need to first understand the underlying theory of *purusha* and *prakriti.* In the Indian *Samkhyan* tradition, *purusha* and *prakriti*, or consciousness and matter, are the two fundamental categories of existence. The world of matter and mind is called *prakriti*, whereas the experiencing individual who interacts with the world is *purusha* or consciousness. Science studies the structure of matter. Physicists and chemists say that matter can be converted into energy and vice versa. Similarly, the *Samkhyan* system says that matter is gross mind and mind is subtle matter and hence they are mutually convertible.

Despite these similarities, *Samkhya* and classical science differ from one another on a very important point. Traditionally, the scientific community has excluded consciousness from their study. *Samkhya* holds that the study of matter cannot be exhaustive and complete without an understanding of consciousness and hence they argue that science is only a partial study of reality. But even the scientific community is now facing the fact that matter and consciousness are interconnected. Take quantum physics for instance. Quantum theory studies matter at the sub-atomic level. They have found that the subatomic particle, the electron, is not amenable to scientific investigation.

When they objectify the electron through observation the scientists discovered that this very observation disturbs the position of the electron and hence the reality of the physical world. And so quantum physics says consciousness participates in the play of material reality. This was discovered long ago by the *Samkhyan* rishis of the Indian wisdom tradition. They said that reality is co-created by *purusha* and *prakriti*, or consciousness and matter/thought. For them, thought is directed energy.

What is consciousness? The answer to this question has to begin with another question: Are we not all conscious entities? The understanding of consciousness depends on the understanding of the conscious individual. Let me explain with an example. The fundamental quality of mind is thinking. In the Indian tradition, thinking has a self-referral quality. As Descartes said, '*I think therefore I am.*' Now take the case of a computer. Computers cannot think, but thinking can be simulated in a computer. You can make a computer 'think' provided you program it correctly. You ask the computer, 'Who is the prime minister of India?' Immediately the computer displays the correct answer. Now ask the same question to a child. He thinks for a while. His human computer also works, and finally he gives the answer. But when he does that, he jumps into the air! There is a sparkle in his eye. There is joy. But does a computer do that? Computers do not jump. Both the computer and the child can compute information. But there is a clear difference between the two. Behind the thinking process of the child's mind we find a conscious entity.

From all this, argue the *Samkhyan*, we understand that there are two fundamental realities which you cannot reduce into each other. You can neither reduce matter into consciousness, nor consciousness into matter. Mental processes can be mechanically replicated, but not the experience of them. According to the *Samkhyans*, mind is part of matter, the inert *prakriti*, and experience belongs to *purusha*, the consciousness. This *prakriti* is composed of the three *gunas -sattva, rajas and tamas.*

The *Gunas* Explained

The *gunas* are energies or modes of matter that constitute the entire material and mental universe. They are *sattva – reflectivity, rajas – activity* and *tamas – stability.*

Because all things are composed of the *gunas*, all things can be categorized and understood by the *guna* theory. For example, the *guna* theory categorizes people into three types according to their *guna* composition.

* A *sattvic* type exhibits qualities of love, caring, wisdom and inner peace.

* A person who belongs to the *rajasic* type exhibits qualities of activity, love of power, domination, ambition, valor, manipulative skills and personal courage.

* And a *tamasic* type is dull, indifferent, stubborn, and inattentive to work and responsibilities.

Similarly, work can be graded into these three types, and even a product can be graded into three. Actually, you can grade anything and everything into these three categories. Even happiness can be graded into three- *sattvic* happiness, *rajasic* happiness and *tamasic* happiness.

- What is *sattvic* happiness? *Sattvic* happiness is the happiness that is painful in the beginning and pleasurable in the end. The example for *sattvic* happiness is spiritual *sadhana* or any type of discipline that is painful in the beginning but pleasurable in the end.
- *Rajasic* happiness is happiness that is pleasurable in the beginning and painful in the end. The example for *rajasic* happiness is the pleasure that you gain from watching a cricket match while ignoring your examination studies.
- *Tamasic* happiness is a delusional happiness that is painful in the beginning as well as in the end. And the example for *tamasic* happiness is the pleasure one gets out of smoking, drinking and substance abuse. The pleasure is delusory.

Knowledge also can be graded into three- *sattvic* knowledge, *rajasic* knowledge and *tamasic* knowledge.

- *Sattvic* knowledge sees the unity of things and people. *Sattvic* people are able to see the connections behind seemingly contradictory forces. When you are able to see the inner connection and the unity of things, that understanding is *sattvic* and synergetic. Take the case of India and Pakistan who are in conflict, both suffering economically and socially in the process. If one can think of a solution by creating a model that can help both Pakistan and India reconcile their differences, that model would be called a *sattvic* model. Such knowledge creates synergy and win-win situations and brings unity.
- *Rajasic* knowledge is that which emphasizes division, difference and conflict. When *rajasic* people read history, they look for facts that suit their point of view and they

create a case for themselves and argue it very well. It is something like two lawyers who argue in a court. They cannot see beyond black and white. They see only their own points of view and keep hammering on. Such *rajasic* arguments are called *vada* in the Indian wisdom tradition, whereas when two *sattvic* people meet their argument is called *samvada*. For the *sattvic* people, the goal is the pursuit of truth and understanding each other.

- According to the Bhagavad Gita, '*Tamasic* understanding is that which is confined to a single object as if it were the whole, which is irrational, exclusivist, not founded upon facts and truth, trivial, and purely selfish,' (Gita 17.22). There is a famous story about Bernard Shaw. Bernard Shaw was on his morning walk and he had to negotiate over a very narrow bridge. Only one person could walk on the bridge at a time. Bernard Shaw was on one end of the bridge, and there was a young man on the other end of the bridge. Bernard Shaw said, 'Sir, please give me the way because there is only room for one and I am old and in a hurry.' The young man at the other end said, 'I do not give way to fools.' Bernard Shaw smiled and stepped aside saying, 'But I do!' The idea is that if there are two good people there are many ways of doing things. If there is only one good man and one bad man then there are only two ways. When there are two bad people, there is only one way- both of them are at each other's throat! This refusal to compromise and understand is the characteristic of *tamasic* people. A *tamasic* person sees only his point of view. *Tamasic* knowledge and understanding are very limited.

Their worldview is highly prejudiced. They have no place for anybody else in their scheme of things.

Here is an easy way to tell somebody's *guna* type. Give a copy of the *Bhagavad Gita* to a group of people and observe how they behave. A *sattvic* person will take the book very reverently, put it in his *pooja* room and read the book every morning. Another person who is *rajasic*, as soon as he gets the book will put a leather cover on it and a stamp on every page and display it prominently in his drawing room. Thereafter he will never even look at it. And what will a *tamasic* person do with the *Bhagavad Gita*? He will try to sell the book or make use of it as a pillow.

Applying the *Gunas* to the Workplace

Jack Welsch, the former CEO of General Electric, says in his book 'Winning' that 20% of the work force of any organization will be extremely smart while the bottom 10% will be extremely dull. He says that winning companies have to engage in an annual blood letting, compulsorily identifying and retiring that bottom 10% of the workforce. This concept of differentiation is applicable in a classroom also. If there are 60 students in a class, 20% of the students will be excellent, 60% mediocre, and the remaining 20% will invariably be dull. It is the top 20% of students who determine the quality of the class. There is a management theory that says that 20% of the people do 80% of the work in any organization and that 20% determine the quality and profitability of the organization. Even in the government, 20% of the employees do the real work while the other 80% of the people make only false claims.

Those who do real work, keep quiet, and do not make any false claims are the *sattvic* workers. What motivates *sattvic* people is the sheer joy of doing their work. They do not want to show off. They feel embarrassed if they are given credit and praise. We have a phrase for such work- *nishkam karma* or self-giving work. *Sattvic* people do their work without personal motives. The people who do big things but make bigger claims and boast that without them nothing will work are called *rajasic*. They do contribute but they want the credit for it. They push themselves and proclaim their deeds. Such people are everywhere. And finally, the Gita describes the *tamasic* doer in the following words- 'An agent who is unsteady, vulgar, arrogant, deceptive, overbearing, indolent, despondent, and procrastinating is said to be *tamasic*,' (Gita 18.28). In the modern parlance, he is the fundamentalist who is willing to cause disruption to society to promote his narrow pigeon-holed values and ideas about God and religion. A person who is basically tamasic has to be trained in social values and responsibilities so that he can fulfill some of the socially productive and useful jobs. Otherwise, without training and education, a *tamasic* person can become very destructive.

Identify the Right Person for the Right Job

You have to guna-analyze people to determine their personality type before you recruit them. It is a vital function of leadership to identify the right person for the right job. Whenever you assign responsibilities to people, try to understand their type and then appeal to their basic personality. If he is *sattvic*, internal values like patience, love, care and sacrifice should be utilized. If he is a *rajasic* person he will enjoy leadership and decision making and controlling others. A *tamasic* person likes to do dull, mechanical work and needs to be told what to do.

When you are looking for salesmen recruit *rajasic* people. They will make a good case for the products that they sell. But when you recruit people for research and development recruit *sattvic* persons, because they have the patience to explore new areas and the insight to be innovative. A *sattvic* worker always thinks of the well being of others and of the collective good. You can leave a *sattvic* worker independent and entrust any responsibility to him. He is a responsible person and cannot do anything wrong. But for the administrative service you have to choose people who know the language of power and manipulation and those who are temperamentally fit for making quick decisions. *Sattvic* people are not suitable for positions of power because of their disposition to see both sides of an issue. When you can see both sides of an issue you become ambiguous and exercise restraint. A leader cannot be like that. A leader has to be able to make quick decisions. Therefore, for high administrative positions *rajasic* people are more suitable. They can make those strong decisions and will not mind hurting and displeasing people. If you have to downsize and restructure your organization and terminate the services of a large number of employees, entrust that job to a *rajasic* person.

And there are jobs where you will need *tamasic* persons. *Tamas* is also an important quality. *Tamas* cannot be avoided. Suppose you have to recruit someone for manning your security gate. Recruit a *tamasic* person who is content with standing the whole day watching people. This is by far the best choice for the *tamasic*.

As a recruiter and trainer your job is not to change the *guna* nature of people. You don't have the patience, the energy or the resources. You have only to see the personality type and recruit people accordingly. Then you give them appropriate training and suitable jobs. Nobody is useless in this world. All have got their own uses. There is a saying in Sanskrit, '*amantram aksharam nasti, nasti mulam anaushadam. Ayoga purusho nasti, yojakah tatra durlabhah.*' It means, 'There is no word which has no magical power, and there is no herb which has no medicinal value. Similarly there is no human being who is worthless.' (Vikrama Charitam). There is no lack of good workers. It is good managers who are in short supply. Good managers who can skillfully find the right worker for the right job are scarce. The manager has to discover the physical and psychological disposition of the people, motivate them and place them accordingly.

The Dimensions of Mind

The mind has many levels. It is like an iceberg. What is unseen of the mind is much more than what is seen. Patanjali says that the mind has five levels:

(i) *Mudha* (dull),
(ii) *Kshipta* (wandering),
(iii) *Vikshipta* (agitated),
(iv) *Ekagra* (one-pointed), and
(v) *Nirudha* (still).

The *mudha* or the dull state of mind is *tamasic*, the wandering and agitated minds are *rajasic*, and the one-pointed and still states of mind are *sattvic*. Suppose you attend a lecture for an hour but nothing goes into your head and at the end of the lecture you say, 'I did not understand anything.' That shows that at that point in time your mind was dull. One should avoid doing important things when the mind is dull. The mind can be dull because of overeating, lack of sleep, or lack of interest.

When the mind is *kshipta* or wandering you listen spasmodically. When all others are laughing you suddenly wake up and ask your neighbor, 'What did the speaker say?' One should have a way of bringing the mind back from its wandering. *Pranayama*, exercise and sufficient rest, help.

When the mind is *vikshipta,* agitated or extremely disturbed you are in a neurotic state. You might stand up and shout at the speaker or throw a book or just run out of the lecture hall. In such a state you need counseling or medication.

The other two states of minds are *ekagra* and *nirudha*. *Ekagra* is where you are one-pointed and your mind moves like an arrow. All that you hear and read goes straight into your head. You understand everything clearly. The last level of mind is *nirudha*. *Nirudha* means alert. In that state creative ideas manifest and the mind is open to all that is happening in the world and it understands things integrally. In our tradition there are disciplines to create these last two states of mind, *ekagra* and *nirudha,* and avoid the three negative states. Unfortunately, this rich tradition of ours remains unknown to our youngsters.

Patanjali continues that there are also five limitations under which the mind functions. An ordinary human being works under these mental limitations, or *kleshas*. These limitations are:

(i) *avidya* (self ignorance),

(ii) *asmita* (ego),

(iii) *raga* (extreme likes)

(iv) *dwesha* (extreme dislikes) and

(v) *abhinivesa* (extreme attachment).

All of our personal philosophies and our entire body of knowledge are built on this shaky foundation of mental limitations. Asking questions and finding answers build a body of knowledge. These questions and answers are in turn influenced by *asmita* or egoistic identification, which in turn is caused by *avidya* or self-ignorance. Your identification determines your identity. Mainly we are identified with the body, mind and memories that constitute our present identity.

There is a third aspect of the mind that *Patanjali* talks about. We are all in one way or another conditioned beings. These conditionings determine the way we know, interpret and interact with the world. Patanjali calls these mental processes *vrittis*, or cognitions. There are five cognitions:

(a) *pramana* (right knowledge),

(b) *viparyaya* (wrong knowledge),

(c) *vikalpa* (imaginary knowledge),

(d) *smriti* (memory knowledge), and

(e) *nidra* (no knowledge).

Pramana or right knowledge is a cognition that corresponds to the object that it represents. For example, when you see a snake you cognize it as a snake and such knowledge is not negated by further experimentation. Right knowledge leads to right actions and expected outcomes.

Sometimes when you see a person from a distance you think

that he has come to ask you for the 100 rupees you borrowed from him. You run away and hide yourself in the bathroom. When you come out from the bathroom after some time, you discover that the person had come to give you 500 rupees that he owed you. Does it not happen sometimes? This is *viparaya,* or wrong knowledge about a situation, that leads to wrong actions and unpleasant outcomes. When President Bush went into the Iraq war thinking that Saddam Hussein had weapons of mass destruction it was a case of wrong knowledge, leading to wrong actions and unwelcome consequences. As a result thousands of people on both sides died. If Bush, with access to all his intelligence can make such a mistake, what to say of ordinary people! We waste tremendous resources and sacrifice many human lives when labouring under wrong knowledge.

There can also be *vikalpa*, or imaginary knowledge. Imaginary knowledge has no reference outside. It can be very creative, but it can be destructive too. When it is creative, new ideas and products are generated. An imaginative person can visualize his creation and then bring it into existence. But when imaginary knowledge happens to be a result of phobias and neurosis it becomes harmful.

Next is *smriti*, or memory knowledge. Memory knowledge is caused by activated memories. Let me give an example. An old man remembers his college days and revels in those sweet memories. Those memories motivate him to act and he buys a gift to send to his old sweet heart. It gives him immense pleasure. In the management parlance this means a product that subliminally appeals to customers' memories will sell better than products that have no such appeal. Products that sell in India may not sell in America. In India, *Ganga* water can be sold because of the memories and emotions attached to it. You can go to the Himalayas, collect *Ganga* water, put it in bottles and sell. People will buy. But that will not sell in America. A product that excites your memory sells. Knowledge caused by stimulation of memories is so real and powerful that it can determine actions and outcomes.

Finally there is the state of *nidra*, or no knowledge. The state of no knowledge, is knowledge about absence. When you say I don't know Chinese, it means your mind assumes a form without any corresponding object outside or inside. *You should know what you do not know*. Otherwise you may undertake actions for which you are not competent and make a mess of your life. As a matter of fact, what we know is little compared to what we don't know. When a person realizes that there are areas about which he has no knowledge he becomes humble and can begin to learn and grow.

The entire phenomenon of mind is a flow determined by the combination of these three aspects of the mind: the five *bhumikas* or levels, the five *kleshas* or limitations, and the five *vrittis* or cognitions. A person's life is nothing but a series of experiences. Experiences are nothing but the flow of mental modifications.

The Power of the Mind

To be an efficient manager you have to understand the workings of the human mind. Western psychologists like Freud, Adler, and Pavlov had experimented with various theories of mind and come to various conclusions. Their studies have helped management theoreticians in formulating their ideas on organizational and individual behavior. *Rishis,* in India, like Patanjali, Kapila, and Kanada also delved into the functioning of the human mind. They had deep insights into the unconscious (*vasana*), and the collective unconscious (*mahat*), and beyond. They have also developed practical disciplines to tame the mind and unfold the inner potentialities. The *rishis* of yore were masters of the mind. Their insights and techniques can help the modern manager in understanding human choices and in influencing stakeholder behavior.

You as managers and leaders will be called upon to play a leading role in the field of economics, business, politics and other aspects of nation building. A good understanding of the Indian mind will be very critical in this enterprise. You must utilize the great discoveries of the mind made by the Indian *rishis.* I am happy that you are in the human resource department where you study and apply all these practical lessons. The coming century will be the century of the mind and of human possibility. Study India's rich traditions and realize the power of the mind.

4

Work Culture and Team Building – The Yajna Tradition*

The supreme God having created beings with yajna impulses commanded them to prosper by collective self-giving work; for verily such dedicated teamwork is Kamadhenu -a wish-fulfilling cow.

Bhagavad Gita: 3:10

Today's topic is work culture and team building. There is a general feeling that India has no work culture. You may or may not agree with this feeling, but it is prevalent and is true to a large extent. There are many possible reasons for this state of affairs.

1. It could be due to our past colonial experience, when the fruits of your hard labor were taken away by the colonial powers. There was no incentive to work hard or save.
2. It could also be due to the social and economic hierarchy that existed in our society, in which the highest echelons of society had no respect for work and manual labor. The *brahmins* pursued knowledge, the *kshatriyas* pursued power,

---

*Lecture delivered at All India Management Association (AIMA), New Delhi on 11th March 2004.

the *vaishyas* pursued money and the poor *shudras*, sitting on the lowest rung of society, worked hard day in and day out, toiling and sweating in the fields and other menial jobs. Their work was not respected by the upper castes. This has been the work culture in India for some time.

3. The third reason generally attributed to the poor work culture in India is the fact that we don't have a healthy civic sense. We don't care about the society in which we live; we don't care about our neighborhood. We keep our values within our family. We set a good example for our children and teach them the highest virtues, we expect them to be ethical and hard working, we expect our spouse to be honest; but when it comes to our interaction with the government, with the neighborhood, we don't follow the same principles. We don't pay our taxes, we don't file our tax returns, and we don't bother about the traffic rules. We will clean up our backyard and throw the garbage onto the road. This is due to the absence of a healthy civic sense. India has not built enough social assets. These are the three reasons generally given for explaining the lack of work culture in our country.

It is said that we have a 'shirk culture.' Shirking work! If somebody gives you work, you cleverly try to avoid the work or pass it on to somebody else. If nothing is accomplished you will say it is the will of God, but when something is accomplished you are the first one to take credit. We also don't appreciate someone else's good work. Shirking work is the dominant attitude in the society in India today. Somebody told me that India instead of a healthy work culture has only cultural-workers.

Lots of cultural work takes place in India: celebrations, *utsavas*, processions with elephants and colorful umbrellas, dances and throwing of colours. Every day something or other is going on to incite our adrenalin. We feel very good about it. Whenever there is a chance to run away from work we will not be behind anybody in taking advantage of the opportunity. Our center of gravity is not in the work place. We always gravitate towards the lazy environment of the home where we feel comfortable.

We have to change our work culture. We should not feel content with the present situation. If we don't change, we will lag in the globally competitive economy. China has a good work culture compared to India. The US has an excellent work culture. How do we go about making the changes necessary to rise up to that level? Ultimately it is your philosophy that determines your work culture. I remember reading a dispute between two Chinese philosophers, Lao-tzu and Confucius. Lao-tzu said, 'Do nothing. That is the road to peace and happiness.' Whereas Confucius said, 'Do for nothing. That is the way to enlightened life.' and China followed Confucius.

This is what Krishna taught in the Bhagavad Gita: *'karmanyeva- adhikaraste ma phalesu kadachana,'* which means, 'Be active, never be inactive, and don't react to the outcome of the work,' (Gita: 2.47). Never remain idle even for a second. As they say, an idle mind is the devil's workshop. If you do not do anything, then all kinds of negative thoughts come to your mind and you become a negative person. The philosophy of Confucius and the *Gita* of 'doing for nothing' is a very healthy philosophy.

While our economy is opening up and India is becoming more and more integrated into the global economy, we are forced to bring in a healthy and productive work culture. We have to think about a work culture that can help us flourish in a competitive global economy, not just survive in a protected Indian economy. The Indian government is trying to privatize most Public Sector Undertakings and hand over the commanding heights to the private sector. The Government recognizes that it is not their business to be in business. That is the kind of environment we are in, and we have to prepare ourselves. To survive in a global economy we have to build trans-national companies. We have to create a winning mindset and think big. We discussed earlier the need for leaders who can reinvent themselves on an ongoing basis, who can recreate themselves and adapt themselves to changing situations. It is these re-engineered leaders endowed with the skill to manage their internal as well as external environment who alone can inspire necessary changes in the Indian mindset to create a vital work culture and bring India into the era of global competition.

Developing a Healthy Work Culture

The first requirement in developing a healthy work culture is for people to invoke their spiritual potentialities and discover their inner source of infinite energy. When you have high energy or 'hynergy', then alone you really live your life the way it ought to be lived. When your spiritual potential is not contacted you have negative energy or 'negergy.' You are tired and confused. You do bad things and bad things happen to you because you have no real source of goodness and inspiration. Many people in search of fulfillment either smoke or drink. These are cheap techniques employed to access energy, which ultimately rob you further of your depleted resources. But it is possible to tap into a real and lasting source of energy and inspiration. We were discussing earlier the relationship between the material world and the Spirit. In fact, the truth is that the material is nothing but congealed Spirit. When the Spirit is manifest it becomes matter. That is what Indian philosophy says. The whole of creation is manifested *Brahman*-Consciousness. So consciousness is the root of the material world. We can contact that consciousness, that Spirit, and bring forth unlimited resources into this world. Such a process of realizing Brahman, your potential, is called *Samadhi.*

Samadhi is the ability to draw your energy continuously and then apply it in your interactive enterprises. You have to become inwardly quiet like Mahatma Gandhi to live in touch with the Spirit. When he spins on the *charkha* he quietly works. When he participates in the Congress working committee meeting he quietly listens. When he negotiates on the rickety bridge at Naokhali, in the midst of the communal conflict, he quietly watches. All the time he remains quiet. The *Yogavashista* says that 'nothing is impossible for a quiet mind.' Such a mind sees things properly, evaluates and designs responses to situations properly. Not reactions, but appropriate responses. When you have that kind of high level of energy you become an intelligent manager, a creative entrepreneur and an inspiring leader.

Communication and Clear Organizational Goals

What should be the philosophy of the new work culture? Theoretically we know that your workforce should be highly inspired towards the goals of the organization. This can only happen if they are clear about what the goals are. Clear goals are very important for a healthy work culture. The clarity of goals of the company should run all through the organizational structure. This is the second principle needed to develop a healthy work culture. Even the lowest man in the organization should know what the company stands for. Look at Malaysia for example. Every citizen, even scooter drivers and barbers, know 'Vision 2020' is their destiny. Everyone is clear and inspired by the national goal. In every household, tea-stall, barbershop, everybody is talking about Vision 2020. The dream has percolated down to the lowest and the least citizen.

In the business world this kind of transparency and goal clarity make the organization smart. It becomes an intelligent organization. Everybody is contributing to its success. There is a well-defined objective, and there is a healthy flow of communication from the top to the bottom and from the bottom to the top. Otherwise, if the boss keeps the goals of the company private to himself, because he does not want to be challenged or questioned or confronted, his company becomes dumb. That kind of hierarchical structure does not have the strength of the people behind it. It cannot be called an intelligent organization. It can only be called a manipulative organization. Everybody should contribute in designing the vision of the organization. This is very important in creating a productive and competitive work culture.

Inner Inspiration

The third aspect of creating a healthy work culture is that people should be able to inspire themselves. Everybody should feel inspired. Ultimately, inspiration is something which you cannot get from outside. You have to discover it within yourself. I can inspire you by giving you a higher salary, or by putting your photo in the in-house journal, or by giving you an award. These things may carry you along for some time, but those inspirations won't last. If I give you a hundred rupees raise you will feel inspired for one week or one month, but again you become disinterested after a while. 'When will I get my next salary raise?' you will say. If your photo appears in the in-house journal you will take the journal home to show your wife. She will be so happy and will go around showing the magazine to all your friends and family. You are thrilled and you work very hard during that time. But the next month another person's photo appears in the same magazine. That is enough to bring you down. You start saying that he did not deserve it and that the organization is promoting undeserving people. You may also be motivated if you are given an award. But again your motivation is short lived. How many times can you be given awards to keep you motivated?

So friends, motivation is such a value that you have to discover from within yourself. You must be able to enjoy your work. When you enjoy your work, you don't need any other motivation.

These are the three requirements for transforming the mentality of the Indian workforce: contacting the Spirit and accessing the source of infinite energy; establishing clear goals and open communication, and developing inner inspiration. When these three things are in place we will quickly develop a healthy work culture.

Yajna Culture

Do we have any models for creating a healthy work culture? Let us draw from our own rich tradition by exploring the culture of *yajna*. The pre-colonial and pre-Islamic Indian society was a very creative society. If you read 'Al Beruni's India' you will find how developed Indian civilization was in the first century of the second millennium. India was advanced in terms of science, technology, astronomy, mathematics, and engineering skills. It is from the vast depths of India's history that this great gift of the *yajna* culture emerged. I will be describing this ancient Vedic model of the *yajna* so that we can correlate it to today's world. From the wisdom of *yajna*, we will discover new insights and learn innovative methods to help us in developing a healthy and creative work culture.

As you already know, management is culture-specific. It is people centered. If you don't know the cultural ethos of your country you will not be able to inspire your people, especially in a country like India where the people are soaked in tradition and culture. The *yajna* is a central metaphor of Indian society. Once upon a time every household in every village all over India performed *yajnas*. The *yajna* was the central theme around which Indian life revolved. What is the meaning of *yajna* and how can we draw vision and values from it?

For a *yajna* you first set up a *yajnashala- the theatre of yajna*. In the center of the *yajnashala* is a fire pit, or *agnikund*, where the fire is lit. The people who sit around the fire are the *yajamana* and *patni* who organize the *yajna*, and the *rithwiks*, priests and assistant priests. Sixteen priests used to be required to perform a *yajna*. The main four priests are called *brahma*, *udgata*, *hota* and *adhvaryu*. In a *yajna, mantras* are a central feature. Without a *mantra* there is no *yajna*. There are also certain materials or *dravya* that are offered into the fire. The *dravyas* are clarified butter, grain, cooked rice, twigs, coconut shells, sesame seeds and milk.

In addition to these five components – *agni, yajamana, rithwik, dravya* and *mantra* – we invoke the Gods to participate in the *yajna*. There were many Gods in the Vedic period. All these Gods were in charge of various aspects of cosmic activity. The priests sat around the *yajnashala*, meditated on Gods, chanted the *mantras*, and then poured the *havish* and the *dravya* into the fire. By propitiating these Gods the performers of the *yajna* were trying to invoke favorable boons.

What exactly do these *yajna* performers ask from the Gods? Their demands according to the Yajurveda are *vittam* (wealth), *praja* (children), *loka* (comforts), and *yashas* (fame). The purpose of yajna is to create wealth in terms of goods and services and human resources. All that you need for a comfortable, healthy and dignified social life is asked for from the Gods through the *yajna*. The *yajna* follows the principle of give and take. In the Bhagavad Gita, Lord Krishna says, '*sahayajna prajasristva pura uvacha prajapati anena prasavisyadhvam esa vah astu istakamadukh*,' which translates as, 'May the *yajna* become a *kamadhenu*, a wish fulfilling cow, and bless you with all prosperity,' (Gita: 3.10). Through the performance of *yajna* we are seeking to create a healthy, wealthy and creative community. Ultimately, *yajna* is a wealth creating enterprise, wealth that leads to commonwealth. And the potentiality invoked is not only from outside, but also from within the deeper Self of every participant. By propitiating the Gods you are also accessing the deeper potential lying latent within you. Through *yajna*, all your wishes can be fulfilled. These days we say that our limit is the limit of our dreams. If we dream big and work hard, propitiate the divine and inspire the Spirit, nothing is impossible for us.

Yajna means Pooling Resources – Creating Synergy

A *yajnashala* can be compared to a modern factory or workplace. The *yajamana* can be compared to the modern leader, CEO or entrepreneur. The four main priests can be equated to the department heads of Finance, Production, Marketing and HRD. *Mantra* is the technology we use to invoke the Gods of productivity. If you don't know the right *mantra* and use the wrong *mantra*, then you get the wrong results. *Rishis* were the discoverers of *mantras.* They were like modern scientists and technologists. *Rishis* in meditation were the R & D resource of the Vedic period. He discovers new facts and invents new technologies. *Mantras* are formulae by which you create better innovative and quality products. The modern *yajnashalas* are the factories and the work places where *yajnas,* productive activities take place and where work becomes an offering to Gods of productivity. In a *yajna*, many talents have to work together. All these people pool their talents. They work as a team. *Yajna* means pooling of resources and creating synergy. Synergy can be created only by a group of truly self-organized individuals each of whom can contribute uniquely to the whole enterprise. If you aren't contributing to the enterprise you feel like an alien in the organization. You won't feel part of the organization.

Everybody has to contribute. Otherwise, instead of synergy a group only creates negergy.

I remember a story that illustrates this point very nicely. A man wanted a fur coat because it was very cold. He went hunting for a bear. Deep into the jungle with his gun he sighted a white bear and he took aim. Just as he was about to shoot, the bear stood on its hind legs and said, 'Wait, Sir! You are a modern manager. Think in terms of synergy. Both of us can fulfill our needs. You can fulfill your need for a fur coat and I can fulfill mine if we join hands. I am ravenously hungry. My need is food. Let us work together!' The bear and the man came together and after a while the man got his fur coat and the bear appeased its hunger. Who was the ultimate beneficiary in this *yajna*? Indeed, it was the wily bear that ate up the man for lunch.

The moral of the story is, everyone has to be strong, everyone has to contribute something and everyone has to benefit as individuals. Then alone the concept of synergy is meaningful. Otherwise you cannot sustain group work. People are not fools. Before long they will discover, if they are a disadvantaged party in the partnership. Either they become very deceptive or they break the partnership. They create negergy. So we have to ensure that all the people involved in the association or organization are benefited. Hence the *yajna* concept says that resourceful people have to come together and then the pooled energy has to be offered at a higher altar.

What is the highest altar in the modern management litany? The highest altar as you all know is the customer. The customer is God. His satisfaction is your motto and your *mantra*. And remember there are many Gods. When you succeed in satisfying the customer, then your market share will increase and along with that the number of Gods and your profits. Therefore all your activities should be geared towards the satisfaction of the customer. When the goal of the company is the satisfaction of the customer you create a higher level of energy, that I will call hynergy. First is individual integration, which will create energy, and when that energy pools together it becomes synergy and when synergy is offered at a higher altar it becomes hynergy.

Thus hynergy is a very significant principle. Krishna warns that not even for a second you can not remain inactive. As a manager, as a leader, you have to be active in the world. Krishna says, 'Look at me, I am always active.' (Gita: 3.22). The modern yogis also have to be active people, not simply passive meditating people. You have to have a center, a core of tranquility within and from that core of tranquility you must be able to act on the world stage. Your work must become your worship. Krishna in a revolutionary statement in the *Bhagavad Gita* says that *yajna* means performing work with this worshipful attitude. Work itself has to become an offering of the highest order. You can attain *siddhi,* total fulfillment, through the diligent performance of work. It is easy to pluck a couple of flowers or apples from your neighbor's garden and offer them to God. But the real worship should be through your honest and hard labor.

The meaning of *yajna* should be understood in the light of the above definition. It is not simply pouring ghee into fire and worshipping invisible Gods. Instead, it is worshiping and invoking your own potential by hard, honest teamwork. The most important thing is your labour. Your work is the best offering you could make to God. Mahatma Gandhi has said,

'Worship without work is hypocritical.' If you simply worship the Lord without contributing to the world, you lead a life of hypocrisy. The *Bhagavad Gita* also says: '*karmendryani samyamya ya aste manasa smaran indriartan vimudhatma mithyachara sa uchyate,*' meaning, 'Those who enjoy without work are hypocritical thieves.' (Gita: 3.6). So work is the best form of worship according to the *Gita.*

Management Means Wealth Creation

What is the objective of management? Management is the art of utilizing limited resources to create optimal value and satisfaction for the customer. Not only those resources are limited, but also you have to produce results within a given time frame. Since time is limited, management uses the jargon 'deadlines,' known jokingly in management circles as 'deadly deadlines.' If you don't meet those deadlines then you are in a soup. So you have to utilize limited resources within a limited time frame and create optimal value for the customer. That is the task of management.

And what is optimal value? Ultimately, optimal value translates as wealth. This has to be very clear. Your job is to create wealth. Wealth means knowledge, goods and services. And goods and services that have got exchange value. Air is not wealth because plenty of air is available, although in Delhi you could say that clean air is wealth because the air is so polluted. Merely 'use value' is not wealth. Wealth is what has got 'exchange value.' It is through exchange that we create wealth. That is the basic theory of Adam Smith. He says, 'Let there be trade, let goods and services flow from country to country.' If it remains in one country, that is not wealth. It has to go back and forth. Capital, raw materials, people should travel back and forth.

As management people, your God is *artha*, wealth, and in the management *yajnashala*, what you invoke is wealth. Chanakya said, '*arthamoolau dharmakamau*,' meaning 'charity and enjoyment are dependent on wealth.' *Dharma* means social well-being and *Kama* means emotional satisfaction. If there is no wealth you cannot satisfy your *kama*, desires, nor can you satisfy your *dharma*, obligations. Both *dharma* and *kama* require the firm basis of *artha*. So *artha* becomes very important. Without wealth there is no dignity. A person who has no means of livelihood has no respect. We need wealth to lead a comfortable life.

At the end of the *yajna* you get the result, meaning you get profit. Your market share grows or your equity value goes up or your brand value improves. What do you do with those fruits? In the *yajna* concept, whatever results you get you must first share with others. All the stakeholders are to be taken into confidence and the fruits should be shared with everybody. Whatever balance remains is called *yajnashishtam*. That balance belongs to the entrepreneur or the leader. Says the *Gita*- 'If you eat the balance after sharing with whoever is involved in the productive activity, that food becomes *amrit*, nectar for you; if you eat without sharing, what you take becomes veritable poison.' (Gita: 3.13).

You can use the *yajna* paradigm to galvanize the Indian mind. Presently the Indian managers are blissfully ignorant about this concept. We have to revitalize this concept. Krishna reinterpreted this concept in the *Bhagavad Gita,* differing from the Vedic meaning, and gave it a new twist altogether. The concept of yoga is used for integrating your inner psyche, your inner personality. The concept of *yajna* is used to integrate the social energy and then offer it to the higher altar, higher principles for greater wealth and greater prosperity. You can create many *kamadhenus*, which means setting up value adding, value creating organizations by this process of harnessing human resources.

Churning the Ocean of Milk

The same idea of a *yajna* is seen in the metaphor of the churning of the milky ocean- *Sagar Manthan*, the famous *Puranic* story. I hope you have heard that story. If you have not heard it, I would not call you an Indian. To be truly an Indian, these mythical stories have to be heard and understood. The story of the churning of the milky ocean is as follows.

The Gods in heaven became old and decrepit as the result of a curse by Sage Durvasa. Gods are usually very young, agile, healthy and fun-loving denizens of heaven. But their lot fell into bad times. They went to Vishnu, the protector of the universe, for help. *Devas* told Vishnu, 'We have become old and weak because of this curse put upon us. Please help us regain our lost health and vigor.' Vishnu said, 'Do one thing. Churn the ocean of milk. Involve everybody, including the *asuras*. From this you will surely regain your health.' *Devas* said, 'But Lord, the *asuras* are our mortal enemies. They torment us. They will never cooperate with us, nor do we want to be seen with them.' Then Vishnu said, 'You have to collaborate with the demons, though they oppose you. This is a crisis situation, and extraordinary situations require extraordinary steps. You have to swallow your pride. Go to the *asuras* and enlist their support for this gigantic project.'

Before they left, Vishnu warned them that many problems would arise while carrying out this mission. The first problem would be finding an appropriately strong churning rope and churning rod. After much deliberation they decided that Manthara the mountain could be the churning rod and Vasuki, Shiva's snake, could be the churning rope. Vishnu also cautioned them that although the churning of the ocean is to bring out *amrit*, the life renewing ambrosia, there could be serious side effects. Vasuki may vomit deadly poison. 'Therefore,' Vishnu advised, 'make sure that you are not standing on the head side of Vasuki. Make sure that the *asuras* stand on the head side. And how will you entice the *asuras* to stand there? Let me give you a strategy. Tell the *asuras* that they, being inferior, will not be allowed to stand at Vasuki's head and that their place will be at his tail. The *asuras* being impetuous and arrogant will not agree to this proposal. They will insist on being on the head side, and you, after a long debate, will accept the demand of the *asuras*.'

After taking the advice of Vishnu, *devas* went to the *asuras* to enlist their support. Halfway through the discussion the point of who will stand on which side of Vasuki in the churning activity came up. *Devas* insisted that they, being superior, should stand on the head side. The *asuras*, as expected, did not accept this proposal and demanded that they should be the ones to stand at the head. After some time, devas finally gave in to the *asuras'* demands and it was agreed that the *asuras* could stand on the head side and *devas* on the tail side. Finally, after going through all the motions of the discussion, the *asuras* consented to participate in the mega-project of churning the ocean of milk. This is very important to remember when strategizing. Your opponent should feel victorious, but real victory should be yours.

The *asuras* and *devas* collected large quantities of medicinal herbs and dumped them into the ocean of milk and set up Manthara in the middle of the ocean as the churning rod and made Vasuki coil around the great mountain to act as the churning rope. The *asuras* and *devas* pulled the snake back and forth and the great project of the churning began. At one time, Manthara slipped down into the ocean bed and the churning came to a grinding halt. There were cries for help. Vishnu took the form of a turtle, plunged into the ocean and lifted Manthara onto his back. Thus the crisis was averted. There is a great management lesson in this. The mountain slipping down into the ocean illustrates a weak national or corporate will. Not just willpower, but discriminative willpower. Not a foolish willpower, but a willpower born of wisdom. Vishnu comes in the form of a turtle and in supporting the mountain he indicates that the leader should periodically boost the morale of the work force. Though an effective leader delegates power and inspires his work force without interfering or micromanaging, in times of crises he intervenes effectively and sets the train of work back on its rails.

The next crisis happened when Vasuki vomited poison. A large number of *asuras* died immediately from the poisonous fumes arising from the nostrils and mouth of Vasuki. When the poison came out, it was Shiva, the God of destruction, who appeared on the scene and took the poison in his hand and swallowed it lest it wipe out *devas* and all other living creatures.

When Shiva swallowed the poison, Paravati, his consort, fearing that he may die of poisoning, pressed on his throat to keep it from entering his body. Vishnu, fearing that he may vomit the poison, closed his mouth shut. Thus the poison was stuck in his neck and Shiva became known as *nilakanta*, the 'blue necked.'

There is another management lesson in this. In any entrepreneurial activity, some poison is going to be generated. Somebody will have to take the blame for the unpleasant decisions. If you are a brave leader you will be the one to take the blame upon yourself. You will say, 'Whatever good has happened is because of others, and whatever bad has happened is because of me.' When a competent leader does that, it becomes a *bhooshana* or ornament for him. Like Mahatma Gandhi said after one of his *satyagraha* movements had turned violent that it was his 'Himalayan blunder.' Unless you are a real leader you will not be able to take that stand. Gandhiji had the courage to say things like that and we are honouring him even today. The leader should be able to make unconventional and risky decisions when needed and put self on the firing line and be able to say, 'The buck stops at my table.' At the same time, the leader should have the inner resilience not to get affected by the consequences of his decisions, just as the poison he swallowed did not poison Shiva. The leader should emerge stronger and more resplendent after a crisis, just as Shiva became blue necked after swallowing the poison.

The story continues. After the churning was complete and Shiva contained the poison, the resplendent God Dhanvantari emerged from the ocean of milk with a pot of *amrit*. But before *devas* could act, the *asuras* snatched the pot and ran away. Thus another crisis is created. This represents the problem of national wealth under the control of evil leadership. The leadership has to make sure that the wealth that is generated is safely in the care of wise men and women. To set things right, Vishnu took the form of a beautiful damsel and went to the *asuras* and managed to bring the pot of nectar back where he entrusted it to *devas*. There is the great management and leadership lesson in this episode, that not only should we create wealth but wealth should be under the custody of enlightened leadership.

Even after devas got the amrit there were still problems to deal with. Once you create wealth, how do you distribute it? People have a tendency to grab the wealth. How do you ensure equitable distribution of wealth? That also is a leader's responsibility. Actually, once wealth is created, equitable distribution becomes another major problem. But before thinking about the distribution of wealth, it is wiser to create wealth first. That is the mistake the erstwhile Soviet Union made. They thought of distributing wealth before creating it and what happened? They collectivized all the farmsteads, the agricultural production went down as a result and ultimately what they ended up was distributing poverty. That is like putting the horse behind the cart. So the first priority should be creation of wealth.

I find a wealth of management ideas hidden in this great mythological story from the Puranas. Modern managers should read this story with an open mind and find lessons they can apply in their daily management tasks. If you can incorporate this metaphor practically I am sure you will be able to galvanize the whole of Indian society. Indian people can relate to these kinds of stories, as this is the lingua and the vocabulary of our country. We must create a new work culture for India so that

India can contribute competitively in the creation of values, goods and services on a global scale. Thus India can become a unique and independent center of world civilization and effectively participate in the global process. As entrepreneurs and leaders in our country's expanding economy, this task is your responsibility.

5

Mindset for Managerial Effectiveness*

Where there is Sri Krishna, contemplative consciousness and Partha, a leader of action, there is sure fortune, victory, prosperity and justice – Such is my conviction.

Bhagavad Gita: 18:78

There was a time when the whole of India was booming with the sound of *mantras* and was alive with the light of *yajnas.* In the *yajna*, people with diverse talents came together. They were people with body and mind integrated by *tapas* (austerity). They created synergy by pooling their talents, which they offered to a higher altar. By this mutual cherishing and nourishing they were able to create an atmosphere of plenty, a *kamadhenu*. That was the word used in the *Bhagavad Gita. Kamadhenu* means a wish-fulfilling cow. Whatever you wish as an individual, or as a society, or as an economy you are able to make it real by this act of mutual cherishing. Through this *yajna* sprit we can grow on a sustained basis and create greater wealth.

---

*Lecture delivered at All India Management Association (AIMA) New Delhi on 17th March 2004.

We need to have a firm basis in our own wisdom tradition to create such a culture in the modern world.

Today I will be talking about managerial effectiveness in a competitive global environment. The world has become a complex web or a grand stage and thus a lot of competition has been created. In this environment, unless you are competitive as a nation, as an organization, and as an individual, you will not survive. You will be pushed aside and will have to eke out a living as a slave or a vassal nation.

Darwin said that nature operates on the law of survival of the fittest. That is hard reality. In our tradition we have a saying that the big fish eats the small fish- the *matsya nyaya*. We are conscious of this law of Darwin, that says that only the strongest will survive. Due to chance genetic mutations, some organisms develop a core competence that gives them a competitive edge over other organisms. We don't know exactly how these mutations happen, but these organisms become stronger and more genetically well adapted and thus they are selected by nature for survival. Evolution is based on biological factors and genetic mutations that the organisms have no control over.

But the situation has come when human beings, endowed with consciousness, can make the blind evolutionary process more and more conscious. That is the difference between an animal and a human being. I have yet to see two lions sitting together debating whether they should become vegetarians or not. They are not conscious of what they are doing and they are not comparing themselves with other animals. They don't have the compulsion to make a difference in the world or to themselves.

We, as human beings, on the other hand, are endowed with a

unique consciousness with which we are able to assess ourselves, we are able to compare ourselves with others and we are also able to conceive of and create excellence, beauty and goodness through our power of imagination. These values are latent properties of consciousness. Being conscious individuals, we have to consciously evolve that consciousness, not just let it happen biologically and blindly. We have to, on a periodic basis, assess our competitive status and create benchmarks by which we can measure our progress in comparison with others and with our own standards.

That is why global competition becomes relevant to human evolution. You compete in your community, in your country, but these days you and your country have to compete with the rest of the world. And we are not talking about competing for survival. Competing for survival is not enough. That capacity India already has. India has been surviving for the last seven thousand years. I think it has gone into our genetic makeup. I heard a joke recently that should there be a third world war, after the catastrophic destruction, only the cockroaches and Indians would survive. We have it in our genes, we have that kind of immunity, we can survive in any situation, we are able to adapt to any situation. But that is not enough.

We have to live with dignity, we have to live with competence, and we have to live by creating a difference in our lives. We have to thrive. India has to think in terms of being a great civilization. We have to think in terms of being a superpower. We have to assess ourselves with reference to China, the European Union or the USA. It is not enough that we compare ourselves with Botswana, Singapore, or even Taiwan and Korea. We have to benchmark ourselves against the superpowers. That kind of pride we must have. We have to project the Indian brand out into the world. Without projecting 'India Inc.' we will not be able to survive in the modern world. In the modern world, power is not simply military power. Though military power is very important, the real power now is knowledge power and economic power. Only the nation that is economically strong can survive with dignity.

So we as Indians have to become a proud nation and think of ourselves as becoming a global super-power. I am not trying to pump your ego. I am trying to visualize where India is going to be, let us say, 15 or 25 years down the road. Are we preparing ourselves as managers, as leaders, as thinkers, for the role India is going to be called upon to play in the world? Economists talk about core competence. What is India's core competence? We have competence in software, in technology, in the English language, in science and mathematics, in engineering, in medicine. When Indians go abroad they excel. So we have a strong core competence. We have to identify with that and leverage it to our maximum advantage.

Peter Drucker says that we have to have a strategic vision for the future. What is the strategic vision for our nation? The intellectuals of this country will have to work on this. The government will not create that vision. It is you and I, who have to take responsibility. We have to think and create ideas in the solitude of our libraries, our laboratories, and our homes. The Planning Commission will not create this vision. It has to be created by individuals. It was Adam Smith and people like him who created the vision for the industrial revolution. Unless we are conscious of our responsibility as individuals in creating this vision, we will not make strides on the global scene.

The World has become Complex

There are several factors that have to be taken into consideration when confronting the problem of projecting India on the world stage. The first is the complexity factor. The world has become very complex. Though it has become one web, it is made up of many diverse cultures and diverse traditions. This diversity has to be understood and accepted. A modern manager has to know how to deal with people of all colours from all walks of life and cultural backgrounds. People are also becoming very conscious of their own rights. It is an age of human rights. Even a child is conscious of his rights. You cannot just throw something in front of the child for his morning breakfast and say, 'This is what I cooked, eat it'. The child will not accept such diktats. You have to bend down to the child and ask, 'Would you prefer toast or an egg omelet or cereal or just banana fry?' You have to give all the options to the child. Thus even a child is conscious of his rights. In ancient times you dealt with your worker as though he was only a pair of hands. Still we say, 'I need two hands' or, 'I have five heads' in my factory. What about the mind behind the hands? What about the brain in the head? These days you cannot just dismiss people, nor can you treat them poorly. You have to treat them as a whole human being with mind, emotions, intellect, needs and aspirations and the Spirit. That is the whole structure of an individual with whom we are dealing.

The second factor that contributes to the complexity of

today's world is that information is pouring in from all sides. Even a village woman knows what is happening in America. Recently I went to a village and there was an old lady about 80 years old, and the moment she saw me she said, 'Swamiji, what do you think about the stock value going down?' Stock value! I wondered why this lady was concerned with stock value. Here she is, an 80 years old woman living in a small village, how does she even know what stock value is? Then I found out that her grandson is living in America and when he comes to visit her or writes to her he tells his grandmother all the juicy news about America. So even she has got access to information. This is the kind of situation we are dealing with now.

The third thing that adds to the complexity of the world is change. Things are fast changing. The products in the market today have a short shelf life. People always want the newest and the latest products. There was a time when mass produced goods satisfied customers. Everybody wore the same kind of shoes, the same kind of glasses and the same kind of suits. It is not so now. Every individual needs a customized product. That also adds to the complexity and competitive pressure in the modern world.

In order to survive in such a fast changing world, it is necessary to develop the ability to make split-second decisions. In today's world you don't have the luxury of spending a lot of time reflecting before making a decision. It is something like driving down the highway at 80 or 90 miles an hour with one hand on the wheel and the other hand holding a map trying to figure out if the upcoming exit is the one you have to take. There are cars behind, there are cars in front, you cannot stop, and you cannot pull to the side. If you miss the exit, you will have to go another

20 miles before you will be able to turn around. You have to decide quickly. This is what it is like in the modern world of competition. You need the ability to quickly assess the situation, collect all the data, process the data, and make your decisions without hesitation. If you don't have that ability you will not be able to operate in today's competitive corporate world.

The World of Competition

In India, we are not new to the concept of competition. We have all heard the story of Arjuna who had to compete with all the kings to win the hand of fair Draupadi. Draupadi was the fairest of princesses of that time, and to win her hand, Arjuna had to shoot an arrow through a small hole in a rotating wheel and hit the eye of a bird, and that by looking only at the reflection of the bird in the water. What a tough challenge. Or let us take Lord Rama who also had to win the hand of Sita through a very stringent competition. So competition is not unknown to us.

But somewhere down the road we lost that temper. We lost that fire in the belly, as they say. We have to recapture it. We have to become like the Roman gladiators. We have to compete and win or fight till we die on the battlefield. When I was growing up, I used to hear about the warriors of ancient days. It was said that they should not die with arrows in their back. If you are killed in this way it shows that you were running away from the battlefield. This person died an ignominious death. You must die with arrows through the chest. That showed you were a real hero. That heroic attitude has to be brought back so that we can pull India back up on its feet.

Let us say you are highly qualified from a recognized engineering, medical, or arts and science college. You have high academic credentials. These things show that you are competent. Without showing your competence you will not be hired. But mere competence is not enough. What you need to be effective in today's global environment is, competitiveness. This is a totally different concept. What do we mean by competitiveness? We are not talking about fighting wars or engaging in fistfights. We are talking about competitiveness in the economic field. Ultimately, to compete means to be productive.

Today in India our productivity as individuals, as companies, and as a nation is abysmally low. We say we had a green revolution, but do you know that in India 57% of the land is arable, whereas in China it is only 13%? So India has more arable land than China, but China's agricultural output is twice that of India's. Their productivity is much higher. We also say that we have this white revolution, that India is the largest producer of milk in the world. But what is the population of cows in India? How much milk does the average cow yield? Millions and millions of cows, but giving only just drops of milk compared to cows in other countries. Their productivity is very low. So let us not just console ourselves by citing the green or white or any other coloured revolution. The true revolution will happen when the productivity goes up.

What do we mean by productivity? Productivity is the comparative value of a product generated by a unit of labour. America is a highly productive nation. Japan is a productive nation. We are seeing it in their performance. We have to benchmark ourselves against these countries. Then alone we can know whether we are really productive or not. It does not mean we are not individually competent people. We are very competent. That is why when we go outside the country our productivity level goes up. When we come back to India, our productivity level goes down.

Maybe it is the Indian climate that is responsible. For six months it is very hot and you are sleepy all the time. The other six months are very cold and you are shivering all the time. This must have some impact on people's productivity. It is possible to do something about this problem. We are living in a time when we can control nature to our advantage. That is what was meant when we were talking about the power of human consciousness over evolution. We have the ability to control nature outside and inside. For example, Houston Texas is a very hot place, hotter than Delhi. But there the productivity is high because they have controlled nature. In Houston people have air conditioners and they are able to live and work in a very comfortable environment. We are living in a technological age where we don't have to be victims of climatic change or vagaries of nature. We can control nature to our advantage. In that controlled atmosphere we can bring out our inner potentiality.

Individual Productivity

The productivity concept is not only applicable to large-scale companies and nations, but it also applies to the capacity of the individual. Each individual has to create a mindset where he strives to become not only competent, but competitive as well. As we mentioned before, the difference between competence and competitiveness is your ability to deliver results, to be productive. Competence is what is seen in your curriculum vitae, your C.V. You have so many degrees from so many universities, you have so much experience, and you have proven your competence. But are you able to deliver? That is the question. We have seen so many first rank university students fail miserably when they become college lecturers. They are not able to get along with people, they are arrogant, colleagues avoid them, and they become depressed. Such people don't have what they call 'soft skills,' the ability to work with people, and the humility to listen to others. Regardless of your competence, if you do not have the soft skills you will not be able to compete and as a result you will not be able to deliver results. You must be able to work effectively in a team to be productive. So competitiveness is competence with soft skills. If you don't have those soft skills, the company which recruited you will throw you out in two months time. You are hired, but then soon you are fired.

It is competitiveness what we lack in public sector undertakings. You go to a bank, for example, and meet the bank manager who is highly qualified, a Ph.D. in chemistry or physics. But as you talk with him you can't help but notice the arrogant attitude, the contemptuous look and the disinterest in his work. You don't want to go to him a second time. He does not have the people skills. In order to be effective in business, what matters most is your soft skills, the ability to organize and handle your emotions.

Emotional Intelligence

Emotional intelligence is basically being able to get along with people. That is only possible when you have control over your emotions. What are the basic emotions that drive us? They are, *kama, krodha, lobha*- lust, anger and greed. Anger is a very negative and destructive emotion. Because of anger you dissipate your energy. You lose your capacity to assess situations and respond clearly and creatively. You spoil valuable relationships with your business partners and co-workers. As modern managers, you need to get a hold over your temper. You need a hold over your ego. You have to be humble. Freud said that 90 percent of our mind is used in managing and processing our emotions. Although we consider ourselves to be rational choice makers, in reality man is an irrational, emotional choice maker. The rational thinker seems to be just a dream of the economists. The mind is like an iceberg. 90% of it is hidden in the depths of our emotions. Subliminal and emotional appeals are important when one deals with people.

So what is important is cultivating the people skills, cultivating the right side of the brain, cultivating the feminine values like compassion, humility, understanding, and the ability to listen. That will contribute tremendously to your effectiveness as managers. But that alone is not enough.

Physical Intelligence

If you want to be an effective manager you also need some physical intelligence. The way you hold yourself in public, the way you conduct yourself, the way you dress, the way you walk into a room, are all part of your physical intelligence. Look at Parvez Musharraf, Pakistan's president. He has got a good sense of dress, he is poised, and he walks confidently. Being an army general he had to learn how to develop that kind of presence. Physical intelligence has to be cultivated. The way you conduct yourself, the way you move, your body language, all these play a part in influencing people. Why did Mahatma Gandhi opt for the meager dress of a loincloth? Through that dress he was making the statement, 'I am with you, the people of this country.' As 80 to 90 percent of the people in India at that time were poor and wearing only loincloths, the statement went well with the people and they responded to his call. Thus, you must develop your physical intelligence if you want to become a strong leader.

Spiritual Intelligence

The fourth capability expected of a modern manager is the ability to be self-inspired. This is spiritual intelligence. In a leadership position in the competitive world you are all alone at the top. Everybody will come to you with his or her complaints, but you have nobody to complain to. You have to be like Shiva who swallowed the poison and remained unaffected. You are operating in a field of unstable equilibrium, full of constant change and ambiguities. There is no blue book to which you can refer. You have to be self-sustaining. In order to handle these challenges efficiently and continue coming up with creative and effective solutions you must have the ability to inspire yourself. You must develop a deep faith in yourself. Nobody motivated Mahatma Gandhi, Mao Tse Tung, or Henry Ford. They were self-motivated people. They heard an inner call, the whisper of eternity as they say. And they worked on stormy dark nights, with leaky umbrellas, and they walked all alone, and never looked back. That kind of a self-motivating, inspiring quality is very important for a modern manager. This is spiritual intelligence.

These are the four intelligences that you have to cultivate and integrate: pragmatic intelligence, emotional intelligence, physical intelligence and spiritual intelligence.

Five Mindsets for Modern Managers

Recently I was reading in a management journal, the Harvard Business Review, which said that a modern manager needs five mindsets. I was struck by the similarities between the Indian concepts and the concepts elucidated there.

- The first mindset required of an effective manager is reflection. First and foremost, you have to manage yourself. This is one of the important values taught by Patanjali, *swadhyaya*, or self-study and reflection. You have to tackle the problem of low morale and lack of energy within yourself. If you feel a lack of energy, the only way to inspire that energy is by reflection, by quieting your mind, by expanding your consciousness. The Indian wisdom tradition says that you can quieten your mind by practicing postures, pranayama, prayer and meditation. As a leader, you must be responsible for keeping your sanity. You cannot say that you forgot to take care of yourself. You have to find time for yourself. You have to pull yourself up by your own bootstraps. Nobody else can do that for you.
- The second mindset required of a modern manager is that he must be a master of analysis. You will never be able to manage your organization without being able to think analytically. The nations who are winning the race between nations in this world are those who are masters of analytical skills, such as the Americans, the British, and the Germans. The Americans and English are very cool analysts and that capacity has made them world leaders. That is their competitive advantage. Not that we Indians don't have the capability of developing

analytical skills. Look at the analytical precision and intellectual prowess of our great *rishis.* It is because of their great power of analysis that their writings and teachings have withstood the test of time. But the analytical skill is presently lacking in Indians. Most of the decisions we make are driven by our emotions. We have to develop a kind of practical analysis. We have to give some special effort to developing rational methods of dealing with problems. Take the case of our relationship with Pakistan. We are unable to sit down quietly and analyze the problem and explore the advantages and disadvantages of various courses of action. Instead we react to the situation emotionally. A cool analytical mindset is an important asset for modern managers in dealing with organizational challenges.

- The third mindset required for a modern manager is that, he must be sensitive to society and must contribute something for social asset creation.
- The fourth mindset is the collaborative mindset, in which the manager can assess everybody's needs, collaborate and explore areas of consensus.
- The fifth mindset expected of an effective manager is the proactive mindset, or the ability to take charge, make fast decisions and respond quickly to situations.

You can either be a global manager or no manager. There is no in-between position in a global economy. If India wants to be the best, and if you as an Indian manager want to be on the top, these mindsets are to be cultivated. The second-best will not survive in this world. You need to have ethical, emotional, pragmatic and spiritual intelligence. That is why the Dalai Lama said, 'It is no more survival of the fittest, but survival of the wisest.' Be wise, be a complete person, a whole person, a holy person. That way you can draw from within yourself, face your challenges and bring out the best you have to offer. You can carve out success for yourself, for your organization and for your country.

magnificent spiritual intelligence. [illegible] the Dalai Lama said, "It is no more survival of the fittest, but survival of the wisest." Be wise, be a complete person, a whole person, a holy person. That way you can draw from within yourself, face your challenges and bring out the best you have to offer. You can carve out success for yourself, for your organization and for your country.

6

Ethical Values for Public Administrators*

Renouncing desire for happiness from the world of senses, the one who, O Partha, delights in the Self by the self is said to be a person of steady wisdom.

Bhagavad Gita: 2:55

I am looking forward to a very fruitful interaction with all of you. You all come from the Administrative Services. I remember the statement of Jawaharlal Nehru who said, 'I am the first servant of the people of India.' The etymological meaning of 'administration' is to serve, to minister or to heal. An administrator is a servant or facilitator or a healer. You, as a community, have been trained to serve the people of India. There is no doubt about that. And that is the meaning of education too. Education is preparing an individual to take up public responsibility, to do public good. You, as administrators, have also been trained to promote the common good of people and

*Lecture delivered at Indian Institute of Pulic Admiistration (IIPA), New Delhi on 17th March 2005 to officers attending APPPA (Advanced Professional Programme in Public Administration).

that is why you are put into the positions of power and decision making. You are given the power to serve, not to dominate or extort. That has been the teaching of the Indian wisdom tradition too. Lord Rama had wielded great power. The *kodanda*, his bow and arrow, is the symbol of his enormous power. He did not misuse power for personal pelf or profit. Using public institutions and positions of power for personal benefit is corruption. If we study the example of Lord Rama, whom we look upon as a role model, we find that he used power to promote public good. You, as public servants, should discipline yourselves along those lines. But the fact of the matter is that it is not happening.

Our country is rated as one of the most corrupt countries in the world and we all are responsible for that sad state of affairs. It is not that a developing country has to be corrupt. Countries grow and reach higher states of economic development and power not through corruption but by disciplined teamwork. I meet people, and all of them are concerned about the cancer of corruption that is eating away at the vitals of our country. This dismal condition should not be tolerated. People expect you, the administrative officers, to strive for making India a corruption free country.

One reason why there is corruption is because government employees in service are not getting sufficient emoluments. They have to maintain a decent standard of living, send their children to good schools, which they are not able to do with their present incomes. Whereas a person who is doing a small business or has gone to Dubai or Kuwait, earns perhaps three times or four times more than what you government servants get. So you feel a kind of complex. You think, 'I have passed competitive exams and look where I am. Whereas my neighbour who has no worthwhile qualification, works in Kuwait, his wife and children wear fashionable clothes and expensive jewelries, go on vacation abroad and what do I get out of my service?' Another reason for corruption could be that we are a poor country. In a poor country where fifty percent of people live below the poverty line, one develops a feeling of insecurity and use power as a means for deriving personal advantage. You know that once you are out of power, after retirement, you will be nobody, which is very scary. These may be some of the psychological or personal reasons why we are corrupt.

Corruption is a serious issue and I would like a serious discussion on this at the end of my presentation. I am not going to talk about how corruption can be stopped. I personally believe that India has to be corrupt because that is the only way that we can oil our economy. Our economy is under the unimaginative grip of the state machinery, what they call 'the permit and license raj.' Under this scheme, all private initiatives are stifled. When you put a heavy stone on a growing sapling it grows crookedly, but it has to grow. Similarly, when the government stifles private initiative, people become corrupt. You cannot be very honest in your dealings. Therefore, I think corruption is good economics in a government-controlled economy, though it is bad ethics. Corruption will indeed decrease as the economy grows and government retreats from business activities. It is embarrassing to say such stark truths. Take the case of my servant. I was going through my household accounts. This fellow had swindled some money. I was livid. But then I argued within myself and said how much do I pay him? I am giving him only Rupees 800 a month. A man earning only Rupees 800 a month has to be corrupt. If I don't pay him a decent salary he is tempted to steal money. When he happens to be a servant we call him a cheat, but when he occupies a position of power we call him corrupt. Both are trying to come out of the suffocating atmosphere of poverty and insecurity. I have to tolerate my servant because if I dismiss him I might get another who is more corrupt. Only prosperity can cure the cancer of corruption. Corruption may be a relevant subject for discussion, but I am not going into all that. I just aired my anxiety about what is happening in India.

Work is the Signature of Life

Bhagavad Gita says pursuit of excellence is the highest spirituality. Bhagavad Gita defines yoga or spirituality as excellence, dexterity in work- '*yoga karmasu kausalam*'. You can realize God when you pursue excellence in work. India is a spiritual country. India is known for its spiritual traditions and spiritual values. How do you define spirituality? If you are a shoemaker and produce a pair of excellent shoes, I would say you are touching God. That is not only seeing God, but also realizing your own potentiality. According to the *Gita* we are a storehouse of enormous energy. *Gita* also says that nobody can avoid work. Work is the very insignia of life. If you try to avoid work then somebody will force you to work and you will have to work as a slave. Work gives you dignity and self-respect, and if you put your heart and soul into your work it makes you a healthy person. If that is the reality, the only question is how should we enjoy our work? At this point you are not happy with the work you are doing. Your only thought is to somehow get done with work, go home and watch TV.

Work is your identity. If there is no work you age fast. That is why when you retire you start losing your health. You grow 10 years older just in a matter of one day after retirement. Business people and politicians are very active because they never retire from work. It doesn't matter whether they are doing good work or bad work; what matters is that they work. I see politicians as very healthy. They have flat bellies, they have pink cheeks and healthy looks, whereas you bureaucrats and even some businessmen have potbellies, their eyes are sunken, and they are lost in worrying thoughts. In America you find people do not retire. Even at the age of seventy and eighty, they work. After retiring from Government service they take up a university job, they even enter business, or do community service, but they continuously work. If work cannot be avoided, then it has to be endured. So let us learn to endure work, but the best is to enjoy work.

When we work, what should be the spirit with which we work? According to the *Gita*, you must explore your own potential in and through work. You have enormous potentiality. In the Indian spiritual tradition the *Guru* gives you a *mantra* to chant. And the most common mantra they give is '*Shivoham*', meaning *I am Shiva.* The *Guru* is trying to affect a cognitive change in self-perception. Modern psychologists are walking the path of ancient gurus. They also give you such mantras as, 'Day by day I am getting better and better.' Or 'I am Okay!' When you say such *mantras* you change your self-perception, enhance your self-worth, and experience the world differently. And then you gain the ability to respond to the world creatively. Shivoham is the defining *mantra* of the Indian wisdom tradition.

The quality of your experiences depends upon the quality of your self-image, the kind of software you have inside. If you think this country is corrupt, and that you also will join in the bandwagon, then your thoughts become corrupt and you act accordingly. If you think you can make a difference to what is happening in India, and have that kind of software in your brain, you feel responsible and become capable of making changes to what is happening. Our wisdom tradition says even if 0.01 percent of our population is trained to become *gunatita*, or transcendental people, they can make a difference to society. Indian wisdom tradition divides people into four categories: *tamasik*, *rajasik*, *satwik*, and *gunatita*.

- *Tamasik* people are those who think that nothing will work; they are indifferent to what is happening around them.
- *Rajasik* people think something can be done. They are arrogant, self-centered, demanding, and are power seeking. As long as they are in power they see that things happen, but when they are out of power they see to it that nothing happens.
- *Sattvik* people want to do things, but they do not have that fire in their belly. After the initial efforts they feel exhausted, and retire to the Himalayas and sit in ashrams and chant *mantras* and console themselves with the thought that, after all, 'everything is an illusion.'
- And beyond these three types are the *gunatita* people who make things happen. They are the kind of people that make a difference in the world and have this belief that they have

access to unlimited energy. They will not blame others for their problems.

We need only 0.01 percent of such people in the government and that can make a difference. That is my first proposition. We cannot change everyone. We can only create centers of excellence and a core of excellent people. In your institution itself, if 0.01 percent is *gunatita* type they can definitely create a change. It is only one bulb that lights up a room; it is only one engine that pulls many bogies in a train. Similarly we require only a few people to make a difference in this country. When I came to this Institute, I saw portraits of Mahatma Gandhi, Jawaharlal Nehru and Sardar Patel. These three people alone changed the quality of Indian polity. During post independence years, especially in the 50s, India was respected in the world. If you have this determination that you can make a change, you gain access to spiritual power and you will see the country changing.

Personality Growth is Possible by Helping Others

If your potential is not unfolded, you feel constrained and frustrated. After a few years of service you feel depressed and conclude that 'nothing will work in this country.' Therefore, first change your attitude about yourself. And that depends on your intention. Intention plays an important role in changing attitudes. If work cannot be avoided, the only question is with what intention and with what self-image we come to the work place. When the intention is to work, not for the sake of getting something personally, but to give something, you explore and unfold your inner potentiality. That is what I mean when I say that development is from within. Your intention is important.

From intention comes thought. When your intention is to help the other, you grow and explore your potentiality. By helping others, you are growing yourself. That is what Bhagavad Gita says. Growth is possible only by altruistic activities – *lokasangraha karma*. One has to expand one's area of concern and engage in activity. There are two objectives. One is to help others. Second is to ensure ones own growth by helping others. Your desires, your thought processes and your words and your deeds, all should spring from altruistic intentions.

We talk about lack of character in the country. You cannot change character unless you change the roots. The roots of our self-image are weak. You think that your destiny depends on what you have. Actually, your destiny does not depend upon what you have. Your destiny depends upon *what you are*. If you think that you are what you have, then you always want to have more and you always want to grab and you do not think of giving. The *Gita's* dictum is, 'By possessing you perish, by giving you grow.' When you give you grow like the spring. The more you draw from the spring, the more the spring becomes active. Let me say this again. Right kind of self-image, right intentions, right thoughts, right desires, right words, right deeds, right habits, right character all lead to your true destiny. Your personality has to be built around the foundation of self-knowledge that you are a field of infinite potentiality.

Personality Grows by Confronting Challenges

Personality growth is possible only by confronting challenges. The more challenges you face the more opportunities you have to grow. Our tendency is to run away from challenges, to seek comfort zones and avoid difficult situations. One should always accept challenging situations. I remember a story about Swami Vivekananda. Once Swamiji was going through a forest and he saw a group of wild monkeys and he started running away from them. The monkeys started chasing him and a situation came when he thought that the monkeys might overpower him. Then he thought enough is enough. He turned around and stared at the monkeys. When he stared at the monkeys they tucked their tails and started running away. From that incident the Swami understood that if you run away from challenges, challenges will chase you. When you are stern, then the challenges become opportunities for you to learn and discover your own potentiality.

India has got a great opportunity now. India is on its way to become a great power. Our leaders will be called upon to make momentous decisions. How would you position India in the global context? You are the ones who will make decisions for the country and implement those decisions. The challenges that you face in the future will be very critical. You must prepare yourself to face those challenges. Therefore the mindset has to be such, that more the challenges the better it is. When India opened up the economy we got scared. What will happen? China will flood the market, America will dominate us, and this will be the beginning of neo-colonialism, all those kinds of thoughts floated around. But defying these cynical prophecies, the opening up of the economy has given newer opportunities. The economy is growing in the process. Poverty is declining. India is shining. So let us willingly invite more and more challenges. I should say the bureaucratic mindset has to change. The bureaucratic mind is such that they do not want to face any challenge; they do not want to invite new ideas. We have to change from the bureaucratic mindset to an entrepreneurial mindset.

The Idea of Detachment

Another important idea that I would like to mention is the idea of detachment. That is the central teaching of Indian wisdom tradition. With a detached mind, you can understand and respond to situations objectively and creatively. If there is no detachment we get panicky, we get upset, and then the brain refuses to function. Krishna says, '*yoga samatvam uchyate,*' meaning 'yoga is balance of mind.' That ability is very important because you are daily facing different kinds of challenges and new demands are made on you and you get confused. Politicians will make demands, your boss will make demands, your subordinates will make demands, and when you go home your family's expectations are there to be reckoned with. Therefore there is a lot of pressure on you. You need the ability to keep cool all the time. When you are cool, your mind is in balance, your own inner vitality will be awake. Your own soul will give solutions to your problems.

In this world we are all seeking happiness – *sukha prapti.* What is the ultimate goal in life, whether you are in the government or in private office or in an NGO? Wherever you are, your ultimate objective is to get happiness. Now I ask you a question. Where from do you get happiness? The *Gita* says your happiness is not in people, not in situations, not in things, not in success, nor in money nor in fame. Your happiness is the quality of your Self. Your happiness is your nature. If you seek happiness outside, you will indeed miss it. So stop seeking happiness and start leading a happy life. Be happy all by yourself. When you come as a happy person into the work place, you will bring out your best. Otherwise, even if you are a highly talented person, if you are not inwardly happy, your talents will remain retarded. That is the final advice that the *Bhagavad Gita* gives: *seek your happiness within yourself.*

Concluding Remarks

If you can employ these five principles in your life, you will be a happy person. Understand that you are a field of infinite potentialities; your growth is from inward out, you should always be prepared to face challenges and should not run away from them, you should be detached and your happiness is within yourself. If you employ these five principles you can re-engineer yourself. You can redefine yourself, reinvent yourself and become a very creative and effective public servant or public administrator and create a difference to the society you live and work in. I have only picked up a few pearls from the ocean of Indian wisdom tradition. As administrators, I request you to read the *Bhagavad Gita,* the *Ramayana*, the *Mahabharata*, the *Arthasastra*, *Panchatantra*, and the *Manusmrti* and interpret them to suit the needs of contemporary society facing global challenges.

LEADERSHIP

7

Qualities of a Leader*

The king's happiness is in the happiness of his people. The people's well-being is the king's well-being. A true king sets aside his personal needs and identifies with people's needs.

Bhisma in Santiparva of Mahabharata

A Leader should be Calm and at Peace

A leader, first and foremost, is a calm person. He remains unruffled in all situations. The Sanskrit word for an unshakable person is a*kshobya – the* imperturbable. When you are undisturbed you will bring out the best in you. Every problem comes with its own solution. The solution is hidden in the problem. When you are *akshobya,* you are able to see the problem as an opportunity.

Let me distinguish between *a reaction* and *a response.* A reaction is an uncontrolled response, whereas a response is a controlled reaction to situations. In response you are a master and in reaction you are a slave of the environment. A leader is able to distinguish

*Lecture delivered to MBA students at IIT Delhi on 11th April 2004.

between reaction and response. In the Bhagavad Gita, Krishna's first advice to Arjuna is to keep cool –'*gatasun agatasun cha na anusochanti panditah,*' meaning, 'Wise people do not get upset over events past or present.' (Gita: 2.11). Arjuna was very much upset and disturbed in the battlefield of Kurukshetra because he found it difficult to fight with his own people, uncles, and grandfathers who were on the opposite side. He threw down his weapons saying that he did not want to fight. He wanted to run away into the forest. It was an uncontrolled reaction, what psychologists might call a flight response. Arjuna was extremely disturbed - *vikshubda*. Krishna's advice to Arjuna was to remain cool. Haven't you heard that expression, 'Be cool man!' All over the world wherever you go, they say 'be cool, take a breath, have a drink.' Be cool and then look at the problem. *Antashitalata* or inner coolness is an important value in the Indian wisdom tradition. A leader should never be agitated. A leader can never be overpowered by events. You may call it coolness, self-confidence, faith in God, or faith in oneself.

A cool frame of mind is infectious. When such a person comes into a group, everybody feels cool and quiet. When you are cool and quiet the best of responses comes out of you because then you get access to resources within yourself. We have that creative potential within ourselves, but because of the disturbed state of our mind we are not able to tap into that reservoir of intelligence and energy. Hence Krishna told Arjuna to remain cool. In the Indian culture any teaching or conference begins with a prayer invoking peace. 'Om! *shanti, shanti, shanti*'. Peace Be! Peace Be! Peace Be! Whereas a political meeting starts with the cry, '*kranti, kranti, kranti*' - Violence! Violence! Violence! Unholy elements try to catch fish in troubled waters. Any idea can be sold to an agitated crowd. An agitated crowd is generally dumb. They exhibit only the lowest common factor in human nature. Therefore, be cool and be the master of your world.

Sankaracharya, the doyen of Indian philosophy and a great Vedantic teacher had advocated certain qualities for a leader. He said a leader should be like an ocean. If you put a stone into the ocean, the ocean does not overflow, nor gets muddied nor disturbed. Whereas if you put a stone into a puddle, not only does the puddle overflow but it gets muddied and you are not able to see the bottom. Similarly a wise man or a great and genuine leader is never disturbed by the circumstances. He remains calm like an ocean- *akshobya*. Like Mahatma Gandhi, who was at the center of the storm as he led the mighty movement for independence, fighting against the most powerful colonial nation! In spite of all the troubles and turmoil, he sat calmly in his tiny room in Ahmedabad spinning the *Charkha* with great concentration. He forgot everything else and concentrated on the work at hand. After this meditation he moved into the political potpourri, Congress Working Committee meetings, meetings with Mountbatten or Jinnah or Patel or Nehru, all the while keeping his cool.

Another important quality of a leader is his ability to give attention to diverse aspects of a problem. Those aspects may be contradictory and may not have anything in common with each other, but still he is able to do that because of his inner quiet. When you are not disturbed by the situation and you are actively engaged in the challenges of the day, you are able to emerge stronger and offer unique solutions to problems. You don't have to read a book to find the solution. When you read a book, you are reading only old solutions. Problems are constantly changing and old solutions will not be applicable to new situations. A leader has to offer innovative solutions to new challenges. A leader needs that power, that spontaneity, the innovativeness. Otherwise he can become a consultant. All failed business leaders become consultants.

I heard this funny story. There was a person who was struggling to sleep. He read lots of books on how to get good sleep. The more he read the more sleepless he became. Ultimately he ended up writing a bestseller, 'The art of sound sleep.' Anybody who read the book fell asleep immediately! Unfortunately, the author himself was still sleepless.

Going back to the past is not the solution. Only if you critically review the past with a contemporary mind and take out the nuggets, you will be successful. Otherwise you will be lost in the labyrinth of the past. That is not what we need. We do not have the time or the leisure for that. We need immediate solutions to contemporary problems. After the *Mahabharata* battle, Arjuna, who won the battle and the kingdom and was in a relaxed mood asked Krishna to repeat the *Bhagavad Gita* teaching. Arjuna confessed that he had not been paying adequate attention to Krishna's teachings in the battlefield as arrows were flying, disturbing his concentration. Now he was relaxed and requested Krishna to repeat the profound philosophy. Krishna said, 'Arjuna, I never repeat. If I teach you the same *Gita* now, I will be teaching something new. My teaching was for the specific situation.' Hence, a good leader never repeats. He is always original. He is always unique. Mahatma Gandhi could capture the leadership of the freedom movement from stalwarts like Motilal Nehru, Gokhale and Tilak because of his unique style of leadership. They were all living in marbled palaces, speaking in English, and dressed up like Englishmen. Mahatma Gandhi came dressed up like a villager in a loincloth and talked in *Gujarati.* He spoke the language of *satyagraha.* He introduced new idioms and symbols and metaphors and could communicate with the people through those means. India, being a multi-linguistic country, has the problem of not being able to understand one another through language. We have to have some way of communication. And that has to come from symbols. India is a country of symbolism. Mahatma Gandhi changed his style from the suited booted Mr. Gandhi of the classes in South Africa, to a loin clothed Mahatma of the masses in India so that he could reach out to the poor people.

Last week, I was in a village in the Himalayas, a place called *Sattal.* It is just one hour before *Nainital.* It is a small village with 40 homes of scheduled caste people. I spent four days there with the villagers. The kind of poverty they live in is unbelievable. Animals and humans live together in shanties, not in brick houses. There is no drinking water. They have to go down the hill to fetch water and then they have to carry the water on their heads in tin boxes. The whole day is wasted in fetching water. I did not see anybody having bath. Their clothes are dirty and their children don't go to school. Nearly fifty percent of the children are suffering from TB. You cannot imagine the condition of those people. And mind you, 400 million Indians are living in that kind of poverty and suffering. We must have some empathy for those people. My point is that a leader must be living amidst the people and he must be able to empathize and communicate with the people. I did not speak their language, but by looking at my ochre robe they found it easy to trust me. That's the power of symbols!

Symbols are a very important medium of communication in India, a country of vast diversity. A leader must have this ability to use symbols, 'brand' as it is known these days. Through branding, a powerful idea is easily communicated. For example, Christ lying on the Cross saying, 'God forgive them.' For the last 2,000 years this brand has been selling. Mahatma Gandhi with a loincloth, a toothless smile, and round-rimmed glasses is a powerful symbol in India. All over the world I see Mahatma Gandhi's pictures. Not only in India but also in America, Europe and many other places you find Gandhi's pictures because he is emblematic of something great as he lived a life of poverty, simplicity and sacrifice. When you live that kind of life people believe in you. A leader sets a powerful example and his life is his message; his life is his brand.

A Leader Offers Solutions to Problems

A leader is a person who offers solutions to problems. That is my definition of a leader. There are many kinds of problems that we face today. Problems can appear at different levels in a society. It can be a local problem, it can be a community problem, and it can be a corporate problem. It can be an economic problem, a social problem, a religious problem, a national problem, or an international problem. If you cannot offer solutions to problems you cannot be called a leader. A leader is basically a problem solver.

I remember an example from Alexander's life. Alexander, when he was a teenager, was playing with his friends. One day all the teenagers got together and held a competition amongst them. They wanted to see who could make an egg stand? An egg cannot stand; it always lies on its side. Many boys tried but they could not do it. When Alexander's turn came, he took the egg and crushed it slightly on the bottom. Now the egg stood easily. His friends saw that it was very easy. They said, 'We could have also done that!' But then why did they not think of that before? A leader is one who makes breakthroughs, finds solutions in his brain and applies them boldly. Alexander could spontaneously solve the problem. Before him no one could figure it out. Alexander had the patent right for the solution. A leader must have problem solving gifts.

That is what Rama did. When Ravana abducted his wife Sita he was wondering what to do. Here was a woman who had sacrificed everything for him; she had gone with him to the forest, and stood by him through thick and thin. Rama was a prince and it was his duty to protect the people dependent on him. He failed in his duty towards Sita when Ravana abducted her. To bring her back safe and secure was now his only mission. Rama was in the forest with no resources. The only creatures that he could see in the forest were monkeys. He realized that to fight Ravana he has to organize monkeys into a fit army. Have you ever heard of an army made up of monkeys? Monkeys are very restless creatures. No one has ever seen these restless monkeys quiet even for a second. But Rama organized the monkeys and built up a good fighting army, defeated Ravana and rescued Sita. Thus the mission was accomplished. So was the case with Lord Krishna. He says in Bhagavad Gita: '*yada yadahi dharmasya, glanirbhavati bharata, abhyuthanam adharmasya thadatmanam srijamyaham,*' which means, 'My mission is to punish the wicked and protect the weak,' – (Gita: 4.7.8). A leader lives and works for the promotion of public good. Rama, Krishna, Christ and Gandhi exemplified that idea.

A Leader Inspires and is Self-Inspired

Once you are motivated by such high ideals and objectives, enormous energy manifests in you. A leader can never be tired. A leader is always inspired. When you are motivated and captivated by a high ideal you become tireless. You are all the time on the move. Look at Gandhi, the way he walked from Sabarmati to the seashore. He was 57 years old but he walked briskly without rest. You and I will say, 'I have a headache, I need hot water, I need rest.' Not Gandhi. He was motivated by an ideal. He did not need rest. Rest was rust for him. In fact, a leader is always active all the 24 hours of the day. He is self-inspired.

When you were a baby, you heard your mother saying, 'Baby, you are the most beautiful, you are the most intelligent, you are my darling, etc'. Those words inspired you. But when you grow up, not even your wife will say nice words to you. When you come home tired she may even scold you. Nobody will inspire you or motivate you when you grow up. Everybody will try to pull you down.

I would say that the very meaning of growing up means not looking for approval or inspiration from outside. You may be doing a fantastic job. You may be fighting for a worthy cause. Your ideals may be great. Yet a leader should not look for appreciation; if he does, he may never get it. You must be able to function in an environment of inner peace, inner energy, and once you tap into that energy you require nothing more.

Krishna says in the Gita, 'I have nothing to lose, nor do I have anything to gain, yet I continue to be active.' (Gita: 3.22). Why are you active? You are active only because you enjoy activity. A leader must be able to say, 'I enjoy being active. I enjoy being in the workplace; I enjoy working in a group. I enjoy making a difference in the world.' Today I was reading in the newspaper about Kiran Majumdar, the chairperson of a biotechnology company Biocon. A reporter asked her, 'Why are you working? You have so much wealth. Being a woman men look down upon you. In a world ruled by arrogant men they resist when you try to talk on equal terms.' She said, it doesn't bother her. What motivates her is the desire to make a difference in the world. 'And how do you do that?' her interlocutor continued. She said, 'I make quality products at competitive prices.' She does not say I do *pooja* everyday, or keep fast. What she said was that, as a businesswoman, her supreme goal is to create quality products for the customer's money. She is committed to the customer.

When a customer buys your product, does he bless you or does he curse you? That is the most important consideration for a business person. Customer is God. When a businessperson understands that he or she becomes a person of ethics. Another person may build a temple with the profit that he made by selling shoddy products and cheating his customers. Even though he used the money to build a temple, I wouldn't consider him ethical. The real ethics in business is in delivering quality to the customer. You have to have your own sense of ethics, your own internal sense of beauty and honesty that will lead to quality and excellence. You are not trying to prove anything to anybody. A leader sets his own standards. That is what I would call self-motivation.

Self-motivation is important whether you are a business leader, a political leader or a community leader. Do not expect any motivation or inspiration to come from others. A leader always sets very high standards. When a servant sweeps the room or cleans the toilet he always leaves some dust or dirt in the corners. He overlooks minute details. But when you yourself do it, you will not leave a speck of dust or dirt because you are doing it for yourself. You are motivated to do so. A leader works for public good as though it is his personal work. Followers do the work, as though they are doing for others. For a leader, work is a labour of love.

A Leader has Great Communication Skills

A leader must have great communication skills. Words are not enough for effective communication. Real communication rarely happens through shallow words. Language sometimes hides your true motives and intentions. The leader should have the ability to use simple metaphorical language. Just a simple symbolic act can stir the whole organization or nation. For instance, Mahatma Gandhi lifted a little salt water from the sea and shook the foundations of the British Empire. What a brilliant idea! It was least effort and high in concept with maximum result. When you use words, remember that you can speak a lot and still convey very little. If you use few words you can convey a lot more.

A Leader has the Ability to Organize

Finally, a leader should have the ability to put together teams. In this complex world no individual can shoulder the whole responsibility of an organization. A good leader is one who can bring talented people together. That is what Microsoft does. It is one of the most diverse organizations in the world. That is why Microsoft is growing. You find Indians, Chinese, Koreans, Malays, and Europeans, people with different talents, people who think differently, people with different racial, religious, and cultural backgrounds, all working together. That makes for a very complex organization. As a team leader you have to find a way to bridge differences and diversity and bring people together to achieve a common goal.

A leader has the Ability to Recognize Talent

Unless you attract the best people you will not be able to accomplish great tasks. Take the case of Rama's leadership. Rama's war council met to discuss the strategies of army formation and war. All members spoke voluminously. There was only one person in a corner who did not talk, and that was Hanuman. Sometimes you think that the more you talk the more you shine. That does not always happen. By simply talking you don't shine. Hanuman did not speak much. Rama could tell, 'Here is a real person. He does not speak much, but there is power and self-confidence in the way he sits and in his conduct. His body language speaks.' Rama came up to Hanuman and gave him his signature ring and said, 'Here is the task for you. You can do it.' Hanuman accomplished the mission given to him.

A leader should constantly grow because if he doesn't grow he will not attract people of talent and capability. Growing means thinking out of the box. That is what Rama did when he attracted Vibhishana from the Ravana camp. Everyone said, 'No, this will not work; he is a *rakshasa.* He may have other motives; he may be trying to get vital information from us.' All kinds of doubts were raised. Rama said, 'No, I believe in him. I trust him.' Even a computer can take routine decisions. Put the data in, the computer will bring up the answer. You, as a leader, have to tap into your guts and follow your gut feeling. Then alone will you be able to bring out innovative solutions, especially when dealing with human resource.

A Leader Appreciates his Workforce

Have you heard that story about the squirrel in the *Ramayana*? When they were building the bridge over the sea to Lanka there was a squirrel, which also participated in the work. He would go to the ocean, dip himself in the water and then come to the shore and roll on the sand. A few grains of sand will stick to the squirrel, which he will shed on the worksite. And the squirrel did it with great gusto. The squirrel was hardly noticed and everyone thought his work was insignificant. The monkeys even thought the squirrel was a nuisance. But the great Rama noticed the squirrel's work and lovingly called him aside and said, 'Very good. You are doing a great job,' and patted him on his back. Even now you can see the three white marks on the back of squirrels. Appreciation of other's work is very important. A true leader will be magnanimous in his appreciation of the work of others. He will never say, 'This was accomplished by me.' He will be generous in saying to his co-workers, 'But for you this would not have happened.'

Concluding Remarks

So these are some of the best qualities we see in the ancient leaders of mythical times. Rama, Hanuman, Krishna, Narada, they all had great leadership qualities and determination to accomplish great deeds. Read our scriptures, *Ramayana, Mahabharatha, Panchathantra, Manusmruti, Tirukul*, and *Arthashasthra*. All these texts have profound insights into management and leadership skill building, on how to motivate people and remain self motivated, how to focus on the goal, how to communicate the vision of the organization and how to work in a sustained manner for the success of the mission without losing track of the ultimate purpose of life. When Rama went to Lanka and conquered it, Lakshmana said, 'Brother, let us stay here. Lanka is rich with gold and diamonds.' Rama said, 'Lanka may be golden, but it does not agree with my values. I will go back. For me, my motherland is far greater than gold and glitter.' A leader always stands by his principles, even under extreme provocations and temptations. If you aspire for great leadership, you must read these textbooks and study these great characters. See how they responded to challenging situations. We can get a lot of management lessons from the writings of Valmiki, Vyasa, Vishnu Sharma and Chanakya. Their works will give you great insight and help you become a globally competitive leader.

8

Leadership Lessons from Indian Mythology*

Whatever a great leader does others emulate. Whatever standard the great set for themselves others blindly follow in their footsteps.

Bhagavad Gita: 3:21

Leadership as well as management is highly culture specific and culture is determined by geography, climate, tradition, and a variety of other factors. Hence, when you as management students want to understand the art of management as well as leadership, you must have an idea about Indian culture and Indian wisdom. People are not just machines. You are supposed to interact with people, motivate them, create teams out of them, set goals for them, inspire them and create results. If you are not able to deliver results, you will not be sitting on the chair. You will be kicked out. Delivering results is very important because results decide the success or failure of a company, as well as your own success. You are the select few in the country who get the

*Lecture delivered at the Department of Management Studies, IIT Delhi on 16th March 2005.

best education. You will be called upon to perform great tasks for the company and for your community. You all are being trained to become leaders and the leader is one who takes decisions. That is how I define a leader. A leader is one who has the guts, the clarity about the goal and the knowledge about his people, so that he can make appropriate and optimal decisions. Not only do you make decisions, you work on your decisions, so that within a time frame you produce results. A leader should have the ability and the stamina to organize people to accomplish organizational goals. Just making a decision is not enough. To implement it you need the cooperation, sustained inspired cooperation, of your work force. This means essentially dealing with people, not with machines. One who deals with machines I would call him a mechanic and it is very easy to deal with machines because a machine is programmed to function in a fixed manner. You switch on the machine and it will perform. You can scold the machine, you can abuse the machine, you can even spit on the machine and still the machine will function. Whereas with human beings, you cannot deal as you like. If you abuse a human being, your own worker, if you talk light of him, if you insult him, if you do not respect him then he will not be inspired to work for you and for your goal. If you tell your subordinate or your co-worker, 'Oh, you stupid idiot, do this work.' Do you think he will do the work? He will either not do your work, or he will mess up your work. A human being has this range of possibilities; you can inspire him to work like a Buddha or you can de-motivate him to work like a *buddhu*. It all depends upon your leadership capability.

You are being trained to deal with human beings and in these days human beings are highly conscious of their rights more than their responsibilities, more so because we are living in an independent democratic country. People are conscious of their rights and entitlements and hence you have to appeal to a deeper level of their personality to bring the best out of them and if you fail you will be thrown out, because others are standing in line to displace you. Do you think that there is scarcity of leaders? Of course there is scarcity of good leaders, and of good people, the people who have command over their own minds and their environment. The task that you are being trained for is not just to pick up certain technical skills or an ability to present a paper; you have been trained to become leaders of this country. You must know the great responsibility for which you are being trained for.

I talked initially that leadership is culture specific. Machines have no culture. Human beings have culture. They have conscience and impulses. That is what drives human beings. You should have a way of going sublimely in the human mind to understand it and then motivate it.

I would like to draw some lessons from our own culture. Our own tradition highlights the importance of leadership and how a leader is made. What can we learn from our own tradition? After all, ours is one of the oldest living traditions in the world, Indian civilization is 7,000 years old and it is still alive and kicking. It is not a dead civilization, it is a thriving civilization. An understanding of the culture is a necessary component of understanding the people with whom you are going to work. You have to remember that now India is being projected as a world leader. If you read foreign magazines on economics, sociology and history, you find the world is looking up to India. Recently I read an article in the *Economist* which is published from London which says that by 2050, that means 45 years down the road, India will be the biggest economic power in the world even surpassing China. India's GDP will grow to the extent of 48 trillion dollars, which means four times more than the present American GDP which is around 12 or 13 trillion dollars. That is how they project India. They say India has got the youngest work force in the world today in the age group of 15 to 40. Within another 25 years, India will come on the top of the world.

Recently I was reading a book by C.K. Prahlad where he talks about 'profit at the bottom of the pyramid.' He says that removing poverty and making profit are not contradictory pursuits. You can make profit by removing poverty, meaning poverty removal is good business. Do well by doing good to others. That is his *mantra*. Once upon a time we had this notion that those who make profit must do so by exploiting the poor people or the labour class. That theory has been discarded. A company can do well by doing good to others.

The Three P's

Currently the management theorists are talking about three kinds of corporate commitment – commitment to the people, commitment to the planet and commitment to profit- the three P's. A company has to make profit otherwise it has no business to be in business. You cannot say that because of your altruistic impulses, your company is running into losses. While a company has to make profit to be in the business, to make its profits sustainable, the company needs to have social as well as ecological commitment. Planet means ecology, people means society, and then profit- that is the three P's – the three commitments of a modern company.

You are moving into an era of leadership, where you cannot simply keep making profit ignoring the other two aspects of profit making. To make your company a sustainable company, a great company- that is the word I hear these days- not just a good company, but a great company, you must have these three commitments: sensitivity to the society, sensitivity to the planet or ecology and also an eye for profit. How do we imbibe all these values? I was talking about C.K. Prahlad, and his theory regarding 'profit at the bottom of the pyramid.' He says that by 2030 or 35, the world will require 500 million i.e. 50 crore technicians. The world will also require 200 million i.e. 20 crore engineers. He predicts that all these technicians and engineers, that means 70 crore of engineers and technicians have to come from India. Japan is becoming aged and old because their population is coming down from 150 million to 120 million and within another 20 years or 25 years their population will become about 90 million people. Similar trend is emerging in Europe, Russia and elsewhere. That way our huge population is a blessing in disguise. He says that world will have to draw its workforce and knowledge from India. Are you ready to take up this challenge? The world says, India is becoming a tiger; it is no more an elephant. Earlier they used to compare us to an elephant, an animal which moves with difficulty and for which a 360 degree turn is impossible. Now they say India is no more an elephant, India is a tiger. But what is India's economic status today? Economists are comparing the Indian tiger to the Chinese dragon. Compared to China, India has a lot of catching up to do. Recently there was an article in the *Economist* comparing India and China which says India's foreign reserve is nowhere compared to China's, India's FDI investment is nowhere compared to Chinas, India's foreign trade is nowhere compared to China's, India's social indices are nowhere compared to China's, India's infrastructure is nowhere compared to China's, even India's much talked about IT sector is not all that great, as it has contributed only 4 per cent to GDP and employs only one million people. That article is a little depressing but I read an article earlier, where they have put India on par with China, United Europe and America. It says that India is poised to become one of the four major powers in the world. I feel India has got a great future. If you want India to sit in the Security Council, if you want India to be counted as one of the major powers, India must have economic and military muscle. Otherwise they won't put you in the Security Council; you will not be able to push your products, your ideas or your people into the world.

The Three C's – Concept, Competence and Connectivity

The leadership competence depends upon three things. First is concept, second is competence, and third is connectivity. Unless a leader has innovative ideas and concepts he will not be able to command the respect of his team. He also needs competence to carry out his ideas into palpable products. But the most important quality of a leader is the ability to network talented people from diverse backgrounds all across the world. This is called connectivity. That is why in the American business schools, they hardly teach you business. You spend most of your time in dinner parties and networking with other leaders of business and industry. When you join a company you use all those connections to your own and your company's advantage.

India's Great Tradition

India has got a great future, but it has to be built upon its glorious past. Awareness of a great past makes you self-confident. If you think that your past is not that inspiring, then you develop an inferiority complex. That is what the British did to India. The British taught us that we are fools. If you start thinking that you are a fool, then you act like a fool. If your parents are fools then you must also be a fool. So that is how they silently introduced that complex into our mind. Now we all are behaving as fools. It is time for us to understand our traditions. I do not say that you adopt your past lock, stock and barrel. You must be able to critically examine and analyse your past and take the best and leave the rest. Understanding the past is very important for a leader, because unless you know the people and their culture you will not know their thought process. Gandhiji would have been a colossal failure in Germany and Hitler would have been seen as a *Ravana* in India. He could not have become a leader in India. Gandhiji would not have become a leader in Germany. Having understood this that leadership is essentially a cultural phenomena, let me talk about Indian wisdom tradition.

Emotional and Spiritual Intelligence

Rama was born in Ayodhaya to great and illustrious parents,

Dashratha and Kausalya. Dashratha means one with control over ten *indriyas,* the five sense organs and the five organs of action. When the mind comes under control it attains peace. That is the idea of Rama being born in Ayodhya, the land of peace, to Dasharatha, one with restrained emotions. The modern psychological term for restrained emotions is emotional intelligence, or EQ. Mere IQ is not enough; EQ is also required in leadership. Unless you have EQ you cannot go up the ladder of an organization. IQ takes you there, and EQ takes you to the top. There is another quality of intelligence which is called SQ. SQ means Spiritual Intelligence, the ability to self-inspire, which is again an essential quality in a leader. A leader is a lonely walker; he walks alone. He does not turn around to see how many people are with him. If you want to be a trailblazer, a trendsetter an innovative leader, you must not look for inspiration from outside. On the contrary you must expect constant public watch for even your minor misdemeanors. Unless you are able to weather through all the baseless criticisms and rejections you will not be able to reach the top. That ability I will call SQ, spiritual intelligence. Take for instance Mahatma Gandhi. When he came to India from South Africa he was past 50 and almost toothless. He took upon himself this historic mission of India's independence and look where he reached. Time magazine was searching for their man of the century. They considered Einstein, they considered Franklin Roosevelt, they considered Mao Tse Dong, Ho Chi Minh, Lenin, and even Hitler, and finally they decided on Mahatma Gandhi along with Einstein and Roosevelt as the men of the century. Gandhi weighed only hundred pounds but because of his spiritual force, what he termed as soul force, he galvanized the whole country, fought against a mighty colonial power, and became a first rank leader of the century. That is what I call spiritual intelligence or SQ. Emotional Intelligence is an ability to keep your mind in balance all the time because as you work in this world, success and failure, profit and loss, and praise and criticism are inevitable and you must be able to keep your mind in balance and learn from your mistakes and improve upon your successes.

When *Bhagavad Gita* talked about emotional intelligence the management world said this is nonsense. Now the world of management is accepting this idea of emotional intelligence. When emotional and spiritual intelligence are in place your skills will manifest, otherwise they will not. When these three kinds of spiritual, emotional and practical intelligence are coalescing in one individual he alone can become a great leader. You do not get trained for spiritual and emotional intelligence in management institutions. They tell you how to analyse and process a mass of data, how to make decisions based on cold analysis. But in the process you are damaging your own mind, your own spirit, your own personality because yours is an imbalanced personality. You need training both in managing your mind as well as accessing the spirit which are critical components of modern leadership. Keeping all these in mind let me analyse Rama's leadership.

Lord Rama's Leadership

You all can become Ramas. For that you do not have to wield a Kodanda, Rama's deadly bow and arrow. You can be Rama when you enjoy being yourself. The process of unfolding your power is called manifesting Rama in your life. The very word Rama is very inspiring. Rama means *svasmin ramate iti*, one who revels in himself. *The first step in developing leadership is that you learn to be comfortable with yourself.* You must have a healthy respect for yourself. When you look into the mirror every day in the morning, if you condemn yourself, 'I am not as handsome as my neighbour, nobody is running behind me, I am a useless person,' if that is your self estimate, self evaluation, then you will be bringing that kind of a person into your interactive life. That will be ruinous. Therefore you must begin with a healthy self-appreciation. As long as you are comfortable with yourself, the world will be comfortable with you. Have you not heard that statement? If you are O.K. the world is O.K. If you are not O.K, the world will not be O.K. Not only that you will not let the world be O.K. You become a disruptive person. Rama means one who is happy with himself.

What can we draw from Rama's leadership style? *Rama welcomed challenges.* If he had refused to go to the forest, you and I would not be talking about him today. Instead of going to the forest, he would have put his father in prison like some of the emperors of Mughal India. Rama would have ruled over Ayodhya for some time and died like an ordinary king. It is simply because he took upon himself the challenge and stood by his principles that he is remembered today. A leader must be able to see an opportunity in a calamity. For example, India's population and poverty – India's population is not a calamity; it can be seen as an opportunity. Every mouth that comes into this world comes with two hands and a brain. What India does to bring up large numbers of people above the poverty line will be a great message for the world, which has more than two billion poor people. What we do here will become a leadership lesson for all the leaders in the world. Therefore, learn to see an opportunity in a calamity. Stand by your principles. It may not serve you immediately, but in the long run it is going to save you. This is what I see in Rama's case. Rama goes to the forest and what does he do there? He is a learning leader. Instead of sitting in a corner of a cave and doing *japa* Rama visited all the *ashrams* of the great *rishis*. In those days the *ashrams* were the centers of great knowledge, the *rishis* were creators of knowledge. Anybody who wanted to create knowledge used to retire in the forest, set up a small *kutiya* and lead a contemplative life, reading, writing and disseminating knowledge. It was the concept of a forest university. Even now when you go to America, most of the universities are in the forest. It is only in Indian universities, the first thing you do is cut down all the trees, and then put up some concrete buildings, install air conditioners, further polluting the air. In that kind of environment the brain doesn't work. In such a work environment you become irritable, angry, reactive, and there is no question of generating knowledge. An *ashram* is a place where you can relax and activate your intelligence. When there is trouble everywhere then you can fish in troubled waters. Is it not? Any mischievous idea can be sold in that kind of a situation. It is only in a peaceful atmosphere that the brain can function. So what did Rama do? Rama went around educating himself. He built his knowledge base in the forest. *A leader should have life long education.* He must educate himself on an ongoing basis otherwise in the modern world you cannot become a leader.

Building Coalitions

Another thing I find in Rama is that he was an expert in building coalitions. Even if you are a first-rate sole super power, you need coalitions. In an organization you have to create coalitions of interest. You have to knit different interests, serve those interests and draw your energy from coalesced consciousness. You cannot be an isolated island in the modern organization. Rama built coalitions wherever he went. He made friends with *Guha*, the king of the *Nishadas* – tribals. He made friends with *Sugriva* and *Hanuman,* kings of South India, and even *Vibhishana,* the demon prince. When Vibhishana crossed over, everybody objected to his presence. Even Hanuman said that Vibhishana is suspect, because he comes from the enemy camp. 'They are *rakshasas*, *mayavis* and one cannot trust them,' he said. Rama said, 'No, you have to trust him.' The modern leader must have the willingness to trust people. You cannot be an effective leader unless you have the emotional intelligence to build bridges across diverse interests, to read the other man's mind, to be sensitive to his interests, and help him grow while you also are growing. That is why Rama said to Sugriva, you do my work and I will do your work.

I always used to wonder why Rama needed Sugriva's help because mythology says Rama can shoot an arrow and that arrow will lift Sita and bring her back. Rama had that power. America could have destroyed Iraq 25 times over. Why should America build this coalition? Because that is the modern leadership mantra- *minimum force, maximum result*. That is another definition of intelligence. Stupidity is maximum effort for minimum result.

Intelligence is playfulness. A leader should be playful. Not stiff necked and worried looking. I can give you a simple example of playfulness for minimum effort and maximum result. Once I was locked out from my room. I was going for a Gita lecture, and my Gita book was locked inside my room. I cannot lecture without my book, because I have to recite *shlokas* . I did not know what to do, as the key was inside. I contacted a carpenter and the carpenter said, 'Swamiji I know you are in dire need of that book, I can come in ten minutes but I will charge you a thousand rupees.' My jaw dropped, a thousand rupees! Where will I find the money? But since I needed the book I told him to come soon. He came immediately, looked around and saw a window in my room open and peeped in. He asked me, 'Swamiji can you give me a stick.' Generally I do not keep sticks, but from somewhere, I got a stick. He had a small magnet in his pocket. He took the magnet, tied it to the stick and moved it towards my bunch of keys which he saw lying on the table. He just touched the key and the key stuck on to the magnet and he took it out. In one minute the whole operation was over. I said, 'For this one thousand rupees! I cannot give you thousand rupees because you made no effort at all.' The man said, 'Swamiji you are not paying for my effort. You are paying for my effortlessness.' When you do the least effort, then you are paid maximum. That is the meaning of innovativeness. That is the meaning of creativity. Indian labor is not compensated sufficiently because their work is not productive or innovative, nor is their work extended to the state of playfulness. The leader has to be playful.

Rama had the capacity to build a coalition and make Sugriva work. He said you do my work and then I will do your work.

This is the meaning of synergy. Rama had this ability to synergise diverse human talents. Your company may be a diversified company where people from different countries, different traditions, different cultures work, but how do you manage the diversity and create an effective organization out of that chaos? Rama can teach you fruitful lessons.

Another quality of a great leader is that *he will never complain about his work force.* You and I sit and complain all the time, 'Nobody works and that is why my company is not progressing. That is why nothing gets done.' A great leader will never say that. He never complains about his work force. Look at Rama again. When Sita was abducted, Rama was helpless. He knew that Ravana had abducted her. It would be a grueling task to fight with Ravana and bring back his wife. He has to put up an army, train them, discipline them and march into Lanka to fight against Ravana. It is no easy task. Rama found no man power available. He could not send a message to Ayodhya for he had sworn not to return there for fourteen years. He looked around. He saw only monkeys. Rama thought this is another challenge, and he made the best fighting army out of these monkeys. That is why I say, a good leader never complains about his work force. If you complain about your work force that they are useless people, they will definitely meet your expectation. Let us not do that. They are not useless people; they are only being used less.

Rama could make a Hanuman out of an ordinary monkey. Hanuman was sitting on the *Rishimukachala,* the mountain, doing nothing. Hanuman was an unemployed minister of an unemployed king, because *Sugriva* did not have power and

Hanuman happened to be his minister. Hanuman had nothing to do. He had lost his purpose and his goal. He was sitting there idling. Hanuman recognized the greatness of Rama and Rama recognized the potential of Hanuman and what a wonderful job they did together. We all know Hanuman's glory. Rama could spot talent. He could make a great leader out of an ordinary person. Same was the case with Mahatma Gandhi. He was a leader who made leaders of ordinary people. That is how Rama motivated.

Finally, we must look at Rama's way of rewarding people. *A great leader does not give material rewards.* When Hanuman did all the work and came back, how did Rama reward him? Sita gave Hanuman a necklace. Hanuman took the necklace and threw it away. He felt insulted for being given the necklace. "Is that the worth of my work?' Rama said, 'Hanuman, I have nothing to give you,' he said and embraced Hanuman. When Rama embraced him, Hanuman felt so satisfied. Hanuman was willing to do anything for the sake of Rama. This is true leadership to motivate people by inspiring them subliminally.

This does not mean that Rama will not get angry. He can become terribly angry when the situation needs it. A leader must have the capacity to love and to become angry whenever it is necessary. When Rama was on the beaches of *Rameshwaram*, he was contemplating building a bridge and he needed some help from Varuna, the king of the oceans. Varuna ignored Rama. Rama became angry. Rama wanted to teach him a lesson. Rama took his *Kodanda* and was about to shoot his arrow. When Rama shoots his arrow it never misses the target. Varuna knew that and then he rushed to Rama and begged his pardon. *A great leader must have the power to punish if necessary and he should not hesitate to use it.* If you hesitate to punish the wicked and the erring, nobody will respect you.

These are some of the great lessons that we can learn from Ramayana and the life story of Rama. We have to interpret Rama and use that knowledge contextually. Learn from the past, interpret it and employ it appropriately. Decision making requires such leadership as integrative, compassionate, and proactive as Rama's. If you have all these qualities then I am sure the future of India will be safe in your hands and you will be able to reach supreme heights in your career.

9

Leadership – Conflict Resolution and Decision Making*

Work alone you have the right, but never claim its results. Let the results of actions be not your motive nor be you attached to inaction.

Bhagavad Gita: 2:47

Leadership is such a complex issue that you cannot analyze it in terms of nuts and bolts. The method that I am going to use in this presentation is not structural or thematic, but in the form of telling stories. We are living in a very volatile and changing and complex world. The issues that go into the complexity of problems are different and hence there is no golden rule or a blue book or rules written in stones for leadership. Since problems are changing you have to offer new answers all the time. Old answers are redundant. Old answers might have been effective and fruitful in the old situations. Therefore leadership requires an innate intuitive capacity to offer new solutions.

---

*Lecture delivered at All India Management Association (AIMA), New Delhi on 18th March 2004.

In this context, I would tell you a story, just to highlight the fact that leaders should always be creative, and be looking for new solutions. You might have heard the story of a person who sold monkey caps. He carried monkey caps in a basket and went from his village to the city to sell them. It was a hot day and while walking the long distance to the city, he rested for a while eating lunch and slept under a tree. While he slept some monkeys came down and picked up all the caps. When he woke up he saw that the monkeys had taken away all his caps. How to get those caps back? Those caps were his sole capital, and if he loses them he will be broke. He shouted at the monkeys and the monkeys also shouted at him. He threw couple of stones at the monkeys; the monkeys plucked some fruits and threw at him. He said shoo-shoo and the monkeys also said shoo-shoo. It struck him that whatever I do the monkeys repeat. That was a great management discovery. He thought let me throw the cap that is on my head, and maybe the monkeys will throw their caps back. He did it, and it worked. The monkeys threw all the caps. He gathered them hurriedly and left. One definition of management is: 'management is that which works'. He went back to his home, carried on with his business and as the years rolled by he became old and his son took over. He wanted to tell some home truths about management to his son and told about his experience with the monkeys. After some years his son was carrying a basketful of caps to the market and he came to the same place where his father had taken rest. He slept under the same tree and when he woke up found that the monkeys have taken away all the caps. He was not perturbed and thought, I have got the management solution to this problem. So he took his cap and threw it at the monkeys. But, lo! What happened? What happened was something he had not anticipated. One of the monkeys picked up that cap also and grimaced, "Your father told you that old story, didn't he? My father also told me the same story."

Today everyone knows what is happening in the world. Everyone has mastered the book of old solutions. But what makes a difference is the newness and uniqueness of the solutions. That gives you the competitive advantage. It is not just competence that is required, what you require is competitiveness on a global scale. Global benchmarking. If you are competitive, then alone you can say, I am an effective manager or leader.

What does Indian wisdom tradition have to say about modern management and leadership challenges? According to the Indian wisdom tradition, a leader is one whose actions are motivated by public good – *lokasangraha*. A leader sets aside his personal profit motives and works for public good – *lokasangrahamevapi sampansyan karmakartum arhasi*. – (Gita: Ch 3.20). A person who dedicates his life energy for the pursuit of public good and public well being alone can be called a leader in the strictest sense of the term. The motto of Ramakrishna Mission is, '*atmanastu mokshartham, jagat hitaya cha* - 'for ones own liberation and for the wellbeing of the world'. A leader must be able to combine self-growth with organizational growth. If he doesn't grow himself in the process, then he becomes a sacrificial goat: a good man but alas, good for nothing. You must be able to direct the organizational activity towards the desired goals and in the process secure your own growth. Or else you will become like Former President of erstwhile Soviet Union Mikhael Gorbachev, who unleashed forces of epochal change, but became a victim of his own Perestroika. Such people are not called leaders. They are just unwilling victims of circumstances beyond their control.

I would say that the basic definition of a leader is one who thinks of and works for public good unfolding his potentiality in the process. He matches self-interest with public interest. If you don't grow in the process then at the end of the day, you will say: 'Oh! I did a lot for the country, I did a lot for the organization, but where am I today? What have I got?' You become a bitter and disappointed person in the evening of your life. That should not happen. A leader must be able to combine personal fulfillment with the nation's aspirations, and if possible, the destiny of humanity.

One more aspect of leadership that I would like to share with you is that a leader is a person who is capable of molding public opinion, whose decisions affect people's wellbeing. If your decisions are of no consequence then you are not a leader. I heard this humorous story. 'In my house all important decisions are taken by me, unimportant decisions I leave to my wife.' What are those important decisions that you take? Those are like what should America do in Iraq or what policy should Russia follow in the Middle East, what should Prime Minister Tony Blair have done with President Bush in attacking Iraq?' And what are the unimportant decisions that your wife takes? 'Which school should my children go, or what brand of TV to buy, in which locality we should buy our home. These 'unimportant' decisions are taken by my wife.' But actually these are the critical decisions that affect the quality of your life. The Gita says that whatever standard a leader sets others simply follow, (Gita: 3.21).

A leader is one whose decisions and actions affect the future of his organization and eventually humanity. Therefore, he is ethically responsible for his actions. Ethics deals with private morality and public good. Anything that contributes to the public good can be called ethical. The foundation of ethics is the dictum, 'do unto others as you want them to do unto you.' Whatever you expect from others, the same favours you should extend to them. A leader is ethically sensitive about his actions and their effect on humanity.

Another thing that is important about the leader is that he is capable of taking unpopular decisions, especially at critical times. Mahatma Gandhi after the Chowri Chowra incident called off the non-cooperation movement and said that it was time for reflection and stocktaking. It was a very unpopular decision at that time. But Gandhi stuck to his guns. Indira Gandhi made the definitive decision of army action to flush out militants from the Golden Temple. That was a tough decision for a gentle lady leader. When a leader takes unpopular decisions, the people will find out his motives and the rationale behind them, when the result comes. In our puranic stories we find lots of unpopular or seemingly unethical decisions being taken by leaders. But they owned up what they did and took the responsibility. A leader has to take decision, and own up to the responsibility. A leader should have the ability to build scenarios, the ability to communicate, and he should be very pleasant and smiling and people-friendly.

Rama's Leadership

Let us go through some of the role models. I will be drawing from our own mythology. Let us take the role model of Lord

Rama. Rama is supposedly a very effective leader. The very word Rama means, 'one who is happy with himself.' People sometime wonder, where do these great men and women get their energy, inspiration and enthusiasm? They may be sick, they may be tired, but they keep working all the 24 hours of the day while always smiling. The secret of their energy is that they are privy to a secret source within themselves. A leader cannot function without access to that supreme energy.

I remember a story about Alexander, when he was campaigning in Asia. It was desert area in Iran where there was no water and the troupes didn't have water for days together. They were thirsty. They went all around but could not find water. Finally they got a small quantity of water. They brought it in a jug and gave it to Alexander. Alexander asked the question, "What about my troupes? Have they got water?" The commander said, "Sir, it is with much difficulty we got this water for you. Where is the question of satisfying the troops". Alexander just poured the water into the hot sand and said: unless the last man in my troupe drinks water, I will not drink." That is the kind of empathy and compassion we are talking about. Unless the leader thinks of the lowliest and the humblest in his organization, he cannot be considered a great leader. Rama was such a leader because he had that inner resource. He never got fatigued. He had his own principles.

Whenever you are in conflict or in confusion, only principles can save you. Principles become the touchstone for you to define what is right and what is wrong. Rama always based his decisions on principles. A leader has to ask this question, 'What are my basic principles which guide me in my life?' When Rama was asked by his father king to go to the forest, everybody opposed that decision. But Rama was the only one who did not question his father's decision. Rama always followed his principles. He could have told his father, 'No, no, the people are with me, even Vasishtha, the king's guru himself is with me, Lakshmana is with me, everyone is with me, I am a popular prince, therefore, I will not obey you.' But instead, Rama said, 'Father, I will give up my right to the throne and I will go to the forest to honour your word.' I think that is a principle centered leadership, rather than convenience-centered leadership. It is because of that we remember Rama even today. Rama had that courage of conviction, that great heroism that he was capable of doing impossible things. Strength comes from his roots in principles. He did not even take a minute to decide. It was a split-second decision. Lakshmana told, "No, brother why do you go the forest? Our father is old, and he will die any moment, people are with you, I myself am ready to arrest father and put him in jail." Surrounded by all these temptations, Rama stood firm and said, "No, I shall go to the forest; that is the decision of my father and I am bound to respect the decision of my father."

That is the quality of a good leader. He lives his life abiding by principles. If you have no principles, then you will be deliberating and prevaricating for a long time. And finally, you may avoid making any decision or make a wrong decision. It's like our former Prime Minister Narasimha Rao, who never made any decision in his whole prime ministerial career. When a reporter asked him, he said, "Who told you I never took a decision. The day I was sworn in I made a firm decision, not to make any decision." If you don't make any decision the pity is that someone will decide on behalf of you.

Rama was a great crisis manager and consensus builder. Among the many qualities he had, the important ones are: *smitabhashi*, of pleasing disposition; *poorvabhashi*, of humble disposition; *hitabhashi*, wellwisher of all; and *mitabhashi*, of few words. By studying the life of Rama, whether we regard him as a historical or a spiritual or a mythical character, we get a lot of insights for modern leadership qualities.

Of course, some of us may not agree with all that Rama did. For instance, Rama's treatment of Vali, the monkey king, who was his good friend. Rama knew that Vali had a special power, to draw half the strength of his opponent. As a result, in his encounter with Vali, Rama shot him hiding behind a tree. It was not *dharma-yudha*. In *dharma-yudha* you don't hit your enemy from hiding. You have to attack him frontally. But Rama was not foolish to encounter Vali from the front, as he would have lost half his strength. The American Defense Secretary Donald Rumsfeld once said that truth goes around with bodyguards of untruth. It is a very tricky statement but there is a lot of truth in it. You cannot as a leader remain straightforward always. Sometimes you may have to suppress facts. You may also deviate from the chosen path to realize your goals, especially when you are dealing with unscrupulous felons. But one should take care that these deviations do not form habits. Rama's was not a perfect decision. But I would call it a practical, optimal decision in that particular circumstance. A leader works for optimal solutions, not for an ideal solution. A leader who insists on ideal solutions will never make any decision. The Gita says, *'sarvarambhahi doshena dhumena agni eva avrita,'* mcaning that 'Just as there is no fire without smoke, there is no action without defect –' (Gita: 18.48). A leader cannot always make a decision, which is satisfying to all parties concerned. Some may feel hurt, offended or excluded and it is the leader's job to explain his compulsions and make the hurt as painless as possible.

Optimal Decision Making - Krishna's Leadership

Let us take some examples from the Mahabharata. Arjuna was fighting against Drona. Drona was a great fighter. He himself was the instructor of Arjuna. Drona had some tricks up his sleeves that he had not taught to his pupils. That is the nature of teachers who love controlling their students. Arjuna could not match Drona's expertise in the battle and Arjuna's spirits sagged. It is at that time Krishna said to Dharmaputra, 'you have to do something now. You have to tell a harmless lie.' This is an instance of what they call psychological warfare. Tell lies and confuse your opponent. Drona, when he is confused will lose his focus and you will be able to defeat him. 'Yudhistara,' said Krishna, 'you have to say, '*Ashwathama hataha* – Ashwathama is killed.' Ashwathama is the name of Drona's only son. Dharmaputra refused to tell the lie. He said it was against his conscience and that he was dedicated to a life of *dharma*, whatever its consequences. Sensing the stubbornness in Dharmaputra's voice, Krishna, the great strategist, responded to Dharmaputra's pleas, 'O.K. if you cannot say *Ashwathama hataha*, Drona's son is dead, can you say 'Ashwathama the elephant is dead?' There was one elephant of the name of Ashwathama that died earlier. Dharmaputra considered the suggestion and said meekly, 'That is possible, though it is not ethically right.' Thus, Dharmaputra mounted an elephant and shouted, '*Ashwathama hathah*'. But before he could say '*kunjaraha*,' the sanskrit word for elephant, Krishna took his conch and blew it, drowning Dharmaputra's words. Drona heard the honest Dharmaputra shout on top of his voice that his only son is dead. Drona trusted Dharmaputra's integrity. And as soon as he heard those terrible words he dropped his weapons and sat on the chariot unarmed and crying, 'My only son is dead, why should I fight anymore?' Arjuna, as he was a hero warrior, refused to shoot the unarmed Drona. But Krishna chided him, 'Hit him now, because if you don't hit him now you will lose the battle. It is time for you to act decisively. Unrighteous people do not deserve courteous treatment. Drona is fighting for Duryodhana, a felon. Both must die.' Arjuna understood the gravity of the situation and hit Drona who fell dead.

These are the kind of difficult decisions a leader is called upon to make in critical times. He has no time to prevaricate. Only a leader can do that. Such decisions cannot be programmed into a computer because situations arise out of the blue. A leader should always be sensitive and turn the tide of events in his favor. If he doesn't, circumstances will overtake him. A great leader has to be a master of the circumstances.

In the army you shoot to kill. That is expected even if the soldier happens to be a Brahmin. And once you shoot, you should hit the target. You cannot waste even one bullet. Otherwise you are unfit to serve in the army. You cannot say, 'When I took the gun my hand trembled, I am a pacifist and I work for world peace.' Once you are in the army you are bound to obey the rules of the army. That is your duty. In unforeseen circumstances, one may have to act according to the exigencies of the situation. A leader should take the responsibility for such decisions. If there is a punishment, the leader should accept that punishment also. It is said that when Rama killed Vali hiding behind a tree Rama committed *adharma*. In his next incarnation as Krishna a hunter hit him and the hunter was the reincarnation of Vali. Thus the *karmic* account was squared. Krishna received the blow smilingly. When violence erupted after Chauri-Chaura agitation, Mahatma Gandhi said it was a Himalayan blunder, and he fasted for three days. That is the kind of mettle a true leader is made of.

In Krishna you find great leadership qualities. Duryodhana invited Krishna to address his parliament with the intention of humiliating him. Duryodhana sent a whip to the parliamentarians saying that when Krishna enters the hall nobody should stand up and show respect. They should sit down, yawn and pretend to sleep. Krishna knew the intention of Duryodhana as he had his own secret service agents in Duryodhana's parliament. But still he accepted the invitation as it was a great challenge for his leadership. He looked at it as an opportunity to sway public opinion in his favour. Krishna came to the parliament of Duryodhana. Krishna has a very charming personality, with his curly hair tumbling on his forehead, his hair decked with peacock feather, dressed in yellow silken robes for the occasion. As he entered the hall emitting radiance like a sunrise, everybody stood on their feet and gave him a long ovation. Krishna waved his hand and everybody sat down and he gave his lecture and received thundering applause. Duryodhana was livid with anger. After Krishna's departure he scolded his parliamentarians, "Didn't I tell you not to stand up, haven't I sent you the whip?" Nobody dared to speak. After a long silence one old man stood up and said, "Sir, let me tell you the truth. It is not that we got up, when Krishna came to the hall; you were the first person to stand up. When you, the leader of the House stood up, how could we not stand up?" Krishna won the heart of his enemies by wit and charm. That is the quality expected of great leaders, the ability even to trap the opposition. You cannot resist the charm of a leader like Krishna.

Hanuman – Servant Leadership

Hanuman is a perfect example of a servant leader. He was very focused, very strong and very firm. Initially Hanuman did not volunteer to go to Lanka, but Jambavan came and told Hanuman, "You have the power to accomplish this task." Hanuman agreed and flew to Lanka. On the way the mountain Mainaka came up and told Hanuman, 'Please spend the night with me, rest well, and continue your journey.' What was the answer of Hanuman? He answered crisply, 'When I go on Rama's mission I don't stop anywhere until I accomplish my mission, come back and report to my boss.' Hanuman politely refused the invitation of the mountain friend. On his journey onward he met another obstacle, a *rakshasi* caught him by his shadow and was about to eat up Hanuman. Hanuman did not want to waste his energy fighting with this lady because that was not his mission. Sometimes we do that. We get lost in unnecessary fights, and in the process we may even win a battle but lose the war. Hanuman asked, "What do you want? The rakshasi said, "I am hungry. I want food." Hanuman said, "O.K. Open your mouth." She opened her mouth. Hanuman became bigger. She expanded her mouth further. Hanuman became even bigger. And finally Hanuman became so huge that the rakshasi had to fully expand her mouth. At this stage, Hanuman became very small, to the size of an atom, entered into her mouth and then came out. This is another quality of a leader. He stays focused, avoids unnecessary fights. Wherever he has to bend he bends without breaking. Stoop to conquer, as the war strategists say.

Hanuman went to Lanka, found Sita and came back. He had to report the matter to Rama. He did the reporting with two words. Hanuman said, '*drishta Sita,*' meaning, 'Sita is seen.' These days, the government-appointed Enquiry Commissions' reports run into thousands of pages, and the message gets lost in the verbiage of words. The report of Hanuman contained only two words. All the heroic deeds he did in Lanka were not mentioned because that would have been unnecessary. Brevity and precision are the hallmarks of a leader. The more you speak, the more you confuse and get confused. For a leader it is very important to communicate ideas with minimum words.

When Lakshmana was lying unconscious and the physician said he needs a particular herb from mount Himalayas, Hanuman immediately took off. He reached the Himalayas, but poor thing, he forgot the prescription. Should he go back and take the prescription? But that involved two trips. He should not waste time. He lifted the whole mountain and flew back. This is what I call inspired leadership. An inspired person does not make any excuses.

Draupadi – Feminine leadership

There are lessons for women leadership too. Draupadi was a perfect example of feminine leadership. In fact, the crucial decision to fight the Mahabharata war was taken at the insistence of Draupadi. Most of the men were vacillating. Bhima, Arjuna, and even Krishna hesitated to plunge into a fratricidal war. But Draupadi was insistent that they should fight and retrieve their honour and the lost kingdom. She said, 'I need justice to live in dignity. Look at my loose hair. Bhima, unless I dip my hand in the hot blood of Dusshasana, who abused me in the open court, I won't be binding my hair. This war is inevitable. It is a war for justice.'

Without such feminine determination the Mahabharata war might not have taken place and Duryodhana might have continued to rule from Hasthinapuri. The moral courage to make such great and momentous decisions came from feminine leadership. Draupadi, I should say, was the leader of leaders. She managed these five great men, Dharamputra, Bhima, Arjuna, Nakula and Sahadeva who themselves were great leaders of men.

Types of Leadership

Having said that let me say that the Indian tradition speaks of four types of leadership. They are manipulative leadership, transactional leadership, transformational leadership and the transcendental leadership.

A **manipulative leader** is one who withholds information. He doesn't reveal anything to his followers or his workers. He misuses information, manipulates people, sets one against the other, thus creating an atmosphere of ignorance, mutual suspicion, animosity and terror in the organization so that he can continue to lead. Duryodhana was a past master in the practice of manipulative leadership. This was the leadership of Stalin in Russia. Such dictatorial style of leadership is seen in the corporate world also. But, that kind of leadership neither lasts long nor leaves lasting legacies. That is what happened to Joseph Stalin in Russia. After his death he was disgraced and denounced by his followers. Some other leaders use another kind of tactic to manipulate their people. When the going becomes difficult they pretend ill and try to earn the sympathy of their victims. Temporarily they tide over the crisis, but in the long run people realize the truth. This is the lowest form of leadership.

The **transactional leadership** is one where the leader allows some kind of flow of information. 'Okay, let us sit down and discuss.' But what is his motive? He is trying to get all the information through the discussion. On his part he reveals very little. He gathers all the information in the name of transactional analysis and when he gains all the information, he uses it to control and stifle his people.

The third type of leadership is **transformational leadership.** The leader brings in new ideas, but the purpose is to sideline old leaders and check opponents and rise to the top. And once he comes to the top he doesn't tolerate new ideas any more. That is what Indira Gandhi did. She brought new ideas, nationalized major banks, stopped privy purses to former rulers of princely States, threw out Morarji Desai, but once she got entrenched in power, there was no room for new ideas. So, transformational leadership is only an excuse for reaching the top and then eliminating the enemy. Thereafter there is no transformation.

Transcendental Leadership – the Sanyasi mode

The highest concept of leadership in the Indian tradition is the transcendental-*sanyasi* mode of leadership. What is a *sanyasi* mode of leadership? The needs of a *sanyasi* are very minimal. As he goes up the hierarchy in leadership, he reduces his physical needs. That is what Gandhi did. Gandhi controlled the entire freedom movement by sitting in the sparse room in Sabarmati ashram or the ashram in Wardha. He had few belongings. As you reach the top echelons of leadership you should live like a *sanyasi* and the Indian people will respond to that ideal. After all, we are talking about Indian management. In the Indian culture, the moral integrity of the leader is highly valued. Americans or Europeans may not bother about it. They don't bother whether their President is chasing girls or is having many affairs. Of course, poor Clinton did have to pay for his indiscretions, but the American people re-elected him for a second term as their President. In India leaders don't get such leniency. We respect leaders of high moral integrity, the *sanyasi* model of leadership. One test of integrity is that your needs are minimal, your words are few, you are honest, straightforward, and a man of humility. So that is the transcendental mode of leadership. As you go up, you behave like a *sanyasi*, a kind of observer, and a kind of watcher. You are able to lead without reaction.

Another aspect of a transcendental leader is that he encourages the growth of his followers. That is what Gandhi did. Most of his followers became great leaders like Nehru, Patel, Moulana

Azad, Khan Abdul Gafar Khan, Rajagopalachari and others. Left to them they might not have become so great, but they became great under Gandhi's inspirational leadership. Gandhi never occupied a position. Without occupying any position he held unbelievable sway over people's minds and led his country to freedom.

Another quality of a transcendental leader is that he creates institutions, nourishes them to a certain stature, develops leaders to run them, and then moves to new areas of activity. He is totally detached. He is a *sanyasi* or *gunatita* at heart. A transcendental leader is a person who challenges himself continuously, on an on-going basis; he will not stick to any place or anything. He creates, and then he leaves what he has created. He goes forward and onward. *Charaivedi*, *charaivedi*. Keep moving is his *mantra*. India promotes a concept of transcendental leadership, where the winner sacrifices all he has won at the altar of public good. In the West we see the winner takes all. Kalidasa describes this spirit of self-sacrifice in his famous work *Raghu Vamsa*. King Raghu, in a victorious campaign, conquered all the neighboring kingdoms, amassed huge wealth, and at the height of his glory renounced everything and became a poor mendicant. Nelson Mandela did it. He renounced his presidency for his successor and retired gracefully to lead a private life.

I am sure that in the emerging world, transcendental leadership will be of highest value, because everyone wants to grow, and, in helping others to grow a transcendental leader discovers his very fulfillment. A transcendental leader realizes that his personal growth depends upon the growth of all.

Conflict Resolution

I will try to touch upon the Indian way of conflict resolution. Conflict arises because of limited resources and limitless needs. So many people with so many needs chase the few resources on this tiny planet. The question is how to allocate resources and goods and services among people. What should be the standard and the norms of resource allocation? That is the basic question of conflict resolution. There are four ways of resolving conflicts according to Indian tradition. They are sama - collaboration, *dana* – reconciliation, *bheda* – division, *danda* – force. A successful leader should be capable of using all these methods depending upon the situation. The first method is the best method. If there is a problem or conflict, both the parties should sit together and try to resolve the problem in such a way that both are winners. How do we solve the problem of Kashmir between India and Pakistan? Can we create a solution where both are winners? We need a success, a victory, where there is no vanquished. When your victory is without a trail of blood, then alone that victory will last. You can create such a win-win solution. It requires a *sattvic* intelligence, enormous patience and compassion. It is called the *sama* way of solving problems. After all why are there conflicts? A conflict arises because you feel that your interests are not secured while your counterpart is trying to secure his interests. It is a, 'I lose - you win' situation. Can we create win-win situations? That is what Krishna did before the start of the Mahabharata war. He went to the Kauravas and reasoned: "Why do you fight with Pandavas? You siblings are hundred and one in number; the five Pandava brothers are your cousins. You are powerful and they are valorous. Why don't you both collaborate, why don't you partner up? Together you can win the whole world?" Duryodhana was a small-minded person. He could not understand the spirit of *sama*.

When *sama* does not work, then the next method used is *dana* – conciliation, or engagement. That is what America is trying to do with China. Rather than fighting with China they have adopted the method of engagement and reconciliation. That does not mean that either America or China is surrendering its respective interests. Both of them are trying to maximize their interests. It is a kind of trade off or give and take. You give up something and your opponent also gives up something. This mode of conflict resolution might help in the Pakistan-India conflict in Kashmir. India takes the portion of Kashmir that it occupies and Pakistan holds onto the area of Kashmir that it occupies. I would call it a *dana* mode of resolving conflict. Though emotionally both countries are attached to the whole of Kashmir, an amicable resolution requires that both the parties give up something. That is a kind of trade off involved in the *dana* method of resolving conflict. You don't give up your core interest but you are ready to sacrifice your peripheral interest. But if that also does not work, what is the third method?

The third method is *bheda*, which is creating dissention in the enemy camp and weakening their fighting resolve. How did Krishna apply this method? When Duryodhana refused to collaborate, Krishna said 'Okay. If you cannot give us half the kingdom, give us quarter of the kingdom.' Duryodhana said no. Krishna said, 'Okay. Give us at least five villages.' Duryodhana again said: No. Krishna entreated, 'Give us at least one village, with five houses.' Duryodhana stubbornly refused to give Pandavas even an inch of land. Finally war was inevitable. Then Krishna employed the third method of creating dissention in the enemy camp. How did he do that? He sent Kunti to Karna. Kunti told Karna crying, "You are my son, I was not bold enough to reveal you this secret earlier because I was ashamed of myself. The Pandavas are your brothers. Please join them and turn your anger against the Karuvas.' Karna was the main fighter on Duryodhana's side. When Karna heard Kunti's words, he was so much in turmoil. He could not focus. He forgot his *mantras*. Eventually he was felled in the battlefield. Krishna used the same technique with Bhishma. He sent Dharmaputra to tell Bhishma, "You are fighting with Arjuna and you are the *pithamaha* for all of us and how can you fight with your own grandchildren who grew up in your lap?" Bhishma said that he has no heart to fight this battle. And he himself revealed the methods by which he could be defeated. Krishna got the secret from Bhishma. Bhishma also was killed in the battle. President Bush applies the same principle of *bheda* on those who are opposing his invasion on Iraq. He is rewarding the weak Russia, ignoring the lukewarm Germany and punishing the belligerent France. They all raged against the American policy in Iraq. This is called Bush's policy of divide and rule.

If that also does not work in resolving conflict, what is the last resort? The last resort is the use of force. A leader should be ready to use force, keep his sword sharpened and when he strikes he should strike decisively. A leader, who cannot back up his words with adequate force, will not be counted as an effective leader. But force should be used sparingly.

Friends, these are some of the insights from the Indian wisdom tradition. You can go on elaborating them further. The leaders of Indian industry and Indian economy can learn a lot from our own tradition and create management ideas, models, and an effective vocabulary, so that we can become not only thought leaders of the world but also management gurus for the emerging global economy.

10

Leadership – A Dialogue*

He who performs his duty without attachment to its fruits is a true sanyasi and yogi; not he who gives up social and sacred duties.

Bhagavad Gita: 6:1

Q: Swamiji, what do you mean by leadership? Would you kindly define?

A: *Swamiji*: The word for leadership in Sanskrit is *shrestha* or *neta*. Shresta means an exalted person. *Neta* is one who stands at the head of a group of people. A leader is one who is capable of conceiving ideals and goals and capable of communicating those ideals and goals to a group of people who are ready to work with him for the realization of those goals. These ideals can be political, religious, social or economic. A leader is a self-motivated person. He is inspired by an inner call, he has discovered his inner vocation and has a clear idea of what he wants to achieve in life. He is not purely idealistic. He is very

*Swami Bodhananda responds to the questions on Leadership posed by Dr B P Mathur.

practical and works close to practical problems of the day. A leader is one who is empathetic to the problems of his followers. He is dealing with people with ordinary desires, ambitions and fears. A leader has to be conscious of the problems of ordinary people. He is an exemplary person. He leads by his personal integrity, character and behavior. He is a man of few words and carries conviction with whatever he utters. A leader in the business scenario has to be highly skilled in his profession. He has to have leisure to strategize his plans. He has to be highly effective in communicating his ideas to his workers, to his patrons and to his clients. In short, a leader is a self-motivated person. He is a lonely traveler because what he sees, others may not see. And hence he needs patience and must be rooted in his inner self.

Q: What are the qualities required in a leader?

A: *Swamiji*: The first quality required is self confidence. He must be conscious of his strength and weakness and he must have confidence that he can do and accomplish whatever dreams and plans he has. Self-confidence comes from vision and clarity about the vision. A person who has no vision and is confused cannot have self-confidence. The second quality expected of a leader is compassion. He must be compassionate and loving towards his compatriots and co-workers. A person who is not compassionate has no way of knowing the feelings of others and hence remains aloof and cut off from the people. Compassion is an ability to look at an issue from the other person's point of view. It is also the ability to empathize with the feelings of others. Lord Rama, Buddha, Jesus Christ, Alexander, Napoleon and even modern business leaders were all compassionate people. And without that a leader will not be able to carry his people along in difficult times. Another quality that a leader must have is ability to recognize and appreciate talent. Nobody can work all by himself. You need a talented team of people. It falls upon the leader to recognize talent and give them opportunity to express those talents. A leader should also give them opportunity to train so that they become skilled in whatever field they are working. Having recognized talents of other persons the leader should appreciate their contributions. Those who do not appreciate the contribution of others can never become good leaders. The fourth quality of a leader is the ability to communicate his ideas and relate those ideas to other's needs and aspirations. A leader who is pre-occupied with his own ideas and ideals will not be able to inspire and communicate those ideals to other people.

Q: Swamiji, there is political leadership, religious leadership, business leadership- there is leadership in the army, say a general leading a troop. Is the basic quality required for leadership the same?

A: *Swamiji*: I think the most important quality expected of leader is clarity regarding his purpose, motive and goals, regardless of whether he or she is a religious or a military leader. Clarity gives him energy, inspiration and an ability to communicate his ideas to people. Maybe a spiritual leader requires more inner discipline and stability and he has to grow inwardly all by himself. But other leaders grow together- they cannot grow independently of the people whom they lead. They cannot lead people all by themselves. In that sense there may be a little difference between religious and other types of leaders, but essentially they require the same qualities: clarity regarding motives, intentions, purpose and goals.

Q: Swamiji, what is the quality of leadership mentioned in our scriptures and what is its relevance in modern times?

A: *Swamiji*: In the scriptures we find various instances where leadership quality is mentioned. The Ramayana and Mahabharata are two great epics that deal with war and leadership. In war the leader is not functioning for personal interest, he is ethically disciplined. In Ramayana and Mahabharata we find great characters of Rama, Dharamputra, Bhishma, Arjuna, Krishna, how they struggled with moral and ethical issues in deciding mundane, temporal conflicts, and how they took decisions. Take the example of Lord Rama. He went to the forest where his wife Sita was abducted. He fought with Ravana and rescued Sita. All this he did without compromising the truth. He fulfilled all his duties diligently and conscientiously without regard to his personal suffering. He is ready to sacrifice himself to uphold certain universal principles. When Rama faced the problem of his wife's abduction he had to save his honour and protect the weak against the strong. Rama did not meekly accept the situation. He determined that justice has to be done and he was ready to fight for justice. An epic leader has great clarity about justice and injustice, fairness and unfairness and he is willing to use all resources at his command for the protection of the weak and for securing justice. The third quality of an epic leader is that he does not do anything for himself. All that he does is for the common good. These are three great qualities of a leader in our scriptures, readiness to sacrifice for values and principles, readiness to fight against injustice and readiness to work for the common good.

You also asked what would be the relevance of these heroic qualities in the modern world. The modern world has pygmy leaders. They don't have the stature and grandeur or the depth of ancient leaders. They are living in a world where democratic values have leveled everybody and brought everything to the lowest minimum common factor. When we face great challenges like the Second World War, or the Freedom Movement we find leaders of epic stature like Mahatma Gandhi, Franklin D. Roosevelt or Winston Churchill emerging.

Q: How important is leadership for prosperity and general health of the country. People talk of political leadership in the normal parlance. Does political leadership affect all other aspects of society?

A: *Swamiji*: Political leadership represents the general character of the society. Political leadership has a role in changing and directing energies of the people. But what is more important is intellectual leadership. Intellectual leadership comes from academia, other institutions like religion, family, world of literature, science etc. What is required is an all round churning process by which the quality of society is uplifted. Great intellectual discussions and debates should take place to define goals and ways of realizing those goals. So, that kind of churning should go on. If we think that political leaders are going to uplift the society we are sadly mistaken. Political leaders reflect the trends and needs of the present society. What we need is intellectual leadership to conceptualize the future and mould the present accordingly. Mere political leadership will not be up to that task.

Q: You have mentioned that political leadership reflects the interaction of leadership in other areas such as academia, religion, science, art and culture. We find that presently leadership is not emerging in these areas. What is the reason?

A: *Swamiji*: The possible reason of intellectual inertia could be the foreign rule under which we lived for the last thousand years. Large numbers of people got alienated from the political and intellectual process and they no longer think in terms of being masters of their own destiny. They have developed a visceral dislike for authority and a pathetic sense of resignation and apathy. It is time for us to wake up from this dismal situation. When you look at other countries such as the USA, Japan, China or Korea you find that despite differences and corruption, people have a general sense of direction, which is reflected in all kinds of activities in the society. What we lack is a general sense of direction in the country, and as a result there is no purposeful and meaningful debate either in academics or in the general public. Everybody is trying to protect his turf by stratagems devious and destructive to public good. I don't have an immediate answer for lifting the people from this sense of helplessness. But the democratic experiment, open market economy and competitive values may stir this nation towards greater goals and objectives.

Q: In the political field there is a statement often made that we get the government we deserve or we get the leaders we deserve. On the other hand there is a saying *yatha raja thatha praja*. How do you reconcile the two statements?

A: *Swamiji*: I think there is truth in both the statements. A country which is indolent and illiterate will project such leadership which gives them false consolation and false dreams, and will exploit their insecurity and fears and give them false satisfaction or achievement like what the tribal leadership is doing in Africa or Islamic dictatorship is doing in Arab countries or the Communist dictatorship like that of Fidel Castro or North Korea does. There is no limit to foolishness as far as masses are concerned. Whereas when the level of education, health, and aspirations of people improve they will pull down such leaders and bring another set of leaders like Lee Kuan Yu in Singapore or like the present Chinese leaders. They may be politically autocratic but they have the intelligence and sagacity to give shape to people's economic and other aspirations. I perceive that there is mutuality between leaders and society.

Q: The problem before the country is how to get good leadership. Our freedom movement was launched under the leadership of Mahatma Gandhi. At the time of independence we had leaders like Pandit Jawahar Lal Nehru, Sardar Patel, Maulana Kalam Azad who guided the country during initial years of independence. Why are we not able to get good leaders now?

A: *Swamiji*: I remember Swami Vivekananda's prophetic words that we are moving into the age of *shudras.* There was a time when leadership vested with the religious prophets. Then leadership moved into the hands of warriors, knights and kings. Thereafter we find leadership moving into the hands of economic powers like corporations, huge corporations that engage in mass production of goods. From there leadership moved into the hands of ordinary people, Communist functionaries etc. You find leadership moving from one level to another level. The situation has come where nobody can have absolute power or authority over anybody. Everyone is becoming an independent center of power. In such a scenario we should stop thinking in terms of great leaders like Mahatma Gandhi or Patel. We should think in terms of idea creators, think tanks, institutions, NGO's, universities and schools, individual researchers and thinkers. So it is going to be a collective process rather than individual enterprises. I don't think of great leaders coming and solving the problems. Problems are so complex, change is so fast, information flow is so massive, and no single individual can have a hold of the situation today. So the general level of people should improve and everybody should participate in this process.

Q: Leadership is required not only in the political field but in all walks of life, business, industry, civil services, education, science. It is important that we have a Vice Chancellor or principal of a school of outstanding caliber so that he is able to inspire the students. Why are we not able to produce leaders?

A: *Swamiji*: We do have leaders but we do not have documentation about these leaders. I can think of an Ambani, a Narayanmurti, an Asim Premji, a Laxmi Mittal, or Sachin Tendulkar, Amitabh Bachchan, or Amartya Sen. Nobody has studied these leaders and projected a theory of Indian leadership. In our effort to understand Indian society and create leadership, this is very important. We need to study Indian leadership of the last two hundred years say from Raja Rammohan Roy to Narayanmurty. An in-depth study is to be undertaken on the scale of Vyasa's or Shankaracharya's. Another reason for absence of leadership is that our so-called leaders are not ambitious enough. They are more conscious of their security and image than leading the country. They don't have the vision of a Mao Tse Tung or a Mahatma Gandhi. Leaders in industry should have the vision of building global corporations and to become a Fortune Five Hundred company. If it is art or science they should think of getting the Nobel Prize. Primarily what we lack is scholarship about Indian leadership and ambition *vijigisha* among Indian leaders.

Q: What steps need to be taken to produce leaders in all walks of life?

A: *Swamiji*: The first step should be creation of quality educational institutions like IIT's and IIM's. People should know the importance of excellence. Excellence cannot be universalized or democratized. Excellence needs nourishment, protection and relentless pursuit and training. If you train five percent of the population and inspire them with the idea of excellence, you have taken a big step in creating leadership. The second important point is that leaders should feel that it is their duty to work for the common good and in that effort they should have a right to discipline and demand obedience from the people like a responsible father disciplining his son. He must feel morally right or morally qualified to punish the erring people. Leadership is not for the chicken hearted. Thirdly there should be enough opportunity for all qualified people to move to the top echelons of power and position. Democratic institutions should ensure that. People with quality and hard work should be able to come to the top. If we can ensure these three things, India would soon create a pool of leadership.

Q: You have just returned from USA after spending a few months there. Do you think there is a qualitative difference in leadership in that country? What lessons can we draw?

A: *Swamiji*: Undoubtedly, USA is a superpower and is a leader in research, economic and military areas. The US system is a continuation of European system or what is known as the Anglo-Saxon culture or way of thinking which is rooted in enlightenment values, power of reason, analysis and the ideology of humanism. The Anglo-Saxons have this great analytical ability of breaking down problems into manageable bits and processing them in their brains and then offering workable solutions. They are able to put teams together, set aside their emotions and offer solutions. I think that is a great ability and because of it they are able to dominate the world both in colonial and post-colonial and even in post-communist times. How to analyze a problem, offer solutions and implement those solutions is a great ability. In India due to poverty, perhaps, or due to our old culture, we are steeped in prejudices and biases, emotional conflicts, ego problems, and personal insecurities. Because of these we are not able to apply cool, analytical problem solving skills, which we will have to learn from the Europeans and the Americans.

COMPETITION AND THE GLOBAL MANAGER

11

Managerial Effectiveness in a Competitive World*

Therefore arise and attain fame, and conquering your enemies enjoy a flourishing kingdom. By me alone have your foes been destroyed, O left-handed hero you be merely an instrument.

Bhagavad Gita: 11:33

Competition is a very tricky, though profound, word. It is misunderstood as a tool of exploitation of the powerless by the powerful. But the fact is that competition has brought in unprecedented prosperity and equality in income distribution. Unless you are competitive you have no chance of survival as an individual, as a corporation, as a nation or as a civilization. The word 'competition' means to bring out your potentialities and grow together. The word has lately got a negative connotation; it implies that competition means lack of cooperation, competition means cheating your partners, competition means selling shoddy products and somehow trying to survive. Though such a negative outcome has been attributed to competition,

*Lecture given at Punjab Business School, Panjab University, Chandigarh on 25th April 2004.

the basic meaning of competition is to challenge each other and grow together. This idea is based upon the law of survival of the fittest. If you have to survive in a hostile environment, you have to train yourself to be fit. In the jungle, competition means physical fitness. If it is in a civilized society, competition means knowledge fitness; if it is in the economic field it means high quality products and service to the customer. The word competition gains different meaning in different contexts. Now, competition has gained larger significance in the modern world of global integration.

An Inter-connected World

The world is integrated, capital is moving, technology is moving, and products are going all over the world. What you produce here is sold in the USA or in Europe. What they produce there is sold in India and China. There is movement of goods and services. There is also movement of people. There are 2 million people of Indian origin working in the United States and 200,000 of them are millionaires. There are 2.5 million Indians in UK and there is significant number of Indians working in other countries as well. So there is movement of people, there is movement of products, movement of ideas. The Internet has brought the whole world to your desktop. You can download ideas and information from all over the world, from the universities, from the libraries, from research institutions. And, anybody who has a new idea can put it on the Internet. Ideas are flowing. It is an inter-connected world. The peasants in Orissa or Bengal or Bihar villages can log on to the Internet and find out what is the market for their products in Chicago or London.

So, the world is a well-connected single village. We all are citizens of this world family and therefore competition has become global competition.

It is not enough that you are competitive in Punjab or Haryana; it is not enough that you are competitive in India. You have to compete with China, you have to compete with Malaysia, you have to compete with Brazil, and you have to compete with Singapore. With this level of competition it is not enough simply to be competitive in a local region. That is the significance of global competition. In this globally competitive world people are struggling to find their place, they are trying to garner market share and grow.

Modern wars are fought not with weapons, but with products. If you have quality products, you have nothing to fear from competition. Take China, for instance. It has almost conquered US's consumer market. You can find their shoes, their pens, their toys, their watches, their small calculators everywhere. You find products coming from all over the world in malls or showrooms you visit in USA. You find clothing from Philippines, Malaysia, Thailand, and Indonesia. In such a world where do we stand? Are we preparing ourselves to compete? India is a member of the World Trade Organization. As per the decision of WTO, all protective tariffs will come down soon, and all subsidies given to agriculture and small-scale industries will discontinue. All the crutches will be taken away. Even universities will have to compete. First world universities are wooing third world students with attractive scholarships and other incentives. Then there is facility for distant learning. Sitting here in India you can log on to university teachings in different countries in North America and Europe. In every field you find this competition. Quality products are available and people are informed of the quality and availability of products. You cannot cheat your customers any more. You are no longer operating in a seller's market. It is a buyer's market. Every buyer knows what kind of product he needs and where it is available and at what price it is available. In such a situation, in a globally integrated market, we have to be globally competitive, especially if India wants to play a leading role in the world economy. Indian managers and business leaders have to develop a globally competitive mindset to become global leaders.

We find that the global market has got distinguishing features. One is complexity. Products and processes are no longer simple. Complex processes have to be gone through to produce products. People's knowledge has added to the complexity of the world. The economies have become very complex and there is change taking place all the time. The shelf life of products has become very short due to technological changes and we have to take instant decisions. If you prevaricate, if you postpone taking decision, somebody else will take decisions and your market presence will be wiped off. Technology is a very important factor in improving your competitive edge.

Life Long Employment or Employability?

Once upon a time, we had this consolation that once we have entered an organization, our life is safe. It was lifelong employment like in government service. Once you enter into service you do not have to work, you only have to strike work! You remain like a leech in the organization. That is not going to be the kind of culture that this global competition brings into our country. Unless you work hard from morning till evening, you will have no future. I have seen people all over the world working hard. We have in India this false idea that in America nobody works and there gun toting men with bottles of whiskey, may be a couple of girls dancing around, and having a good time. That is blatantly wrong. They work hard from morning till evening. They eat their breakfast while in transit. They shave sometimes in the train. They are up at about 6 or 7 in the morning, jump into the car, go to the railway station, get into the train and while in the train they attend to some of their personal needs and then after a grueling day of work they come back home only at 8 or 9 PM. They do three part-time jobs. Even at the age of 70 they work. They keep their competitive edge because people are working very hard. Even a PhD student is working in five homes, cleaning latrines. Parents give them minimal support. They have to work to earn a living. Unless our people learn to work hard, from morning till evening, we cannot create a competitive economy or society in our country. So let us not have this notion that when the economy develops you will not have to work. Hard work is the key for any society, if you want to have a competitive edge.

I would like to add that it is not going to be lifelong employment anymore. It will be a hire-and-fire labour policy in a competitive economy. If we want to develop a competitive economy, we have to change our labour laws, where the labourer should know that the reward is directly connected to output. Once this idea becomes clear to labourers they will work hard. We have to say it very clearly. It is not going to be life-long employment like in the government service. Government is going to retire most of their people and step back from business activities. We do not need all these government employees to run this country. The present strength will go down by 80%. Only 20% of the present bureaucracy is necessary to run this country. Yesterday I visited a Khadi Emporium in Delhi. There are hundreds of people swarming around you. There I found more employees than customers. One person is enough to attend to 10 customers, but what I found was 10 employees to tend to 1 customer! What will be the productivity of that business? This is the sad situation in our country. Look at the security the employees are enjoying today in government service. But does that make them honest and productive? It is hire-and-fire policy alone that can create competitive edge.

In our country it is not hire and fire, it is fire and hire policy. Before you recruit, you demoralize him, scold him, call him useless, *gadha hai*, etc. Thereafter like a big uncle you hire him. But in the developed countries it is not like that. First they hire a person, and then give him opportunity to prove himself. It does not matter whether he has all the academic qualifications, it does not matter whether he has the right kind of recommendation. They do not even look at your certificates. They look at your face and ask, "Can you do this job? What can you do?" You have to verbally announce who you are, and if you say, "I can," that is enough. They trust your word and they put you in the job. They will allow you to make mistakes, because they know that it is only by making mistakes you can learn. But if you cannot deliver within three months or six months, they will give you a pink slip. This is the attitude. No strike. Strikes will not work there. When we think of competition, and creating competitive managers, competitive society and economy we have to understand life long employment doesn't jell with competition.

What is possible is life long employability. Every individual is responsible for his own employability. Employability depends upon your technical skill level, your knowledge base, and your readiness to learn on the job, because you cannot learn everything at the university. Your readiness to learn on the job, readiness to update your knowledge, readiness to read, readiness to attend seminars and to learn more will determine your employability. Let us not think of working in the same organization for more than three years any more. After more than three years, even in love, you get fed up with the person you loved! Is it not? The same is with organizations. For three years, you can give your maximum to an organization. After that, either the organization or you will get fed up with each other. The company loses its ability to challenge you and when you are not challenged, you are not learning in an organization. You feel that you have become a deadwood in the organization. Once that feeling comes to you, it is time for you to leave. You must be prepared for that. Otherwise you will become a deadwood and you will be pushed around and you will become unemployable and under-employed and under-productive. You must always prepare yourself, always look for opportunities and if an organization cannot fulfill your ambition, get out of that organization and start something new.

In a developed country, 80 percent of the economy is in the service sector. In a developing country like India 50-60% of our GDP comes from the service sector. So it is not big companies alone that produce wealth. Millions of small partnerships or individual enterprises also produce wealth. You can start small industries on your own. What is important is developing the entrepreneurial interest and initiative in the people. You must make every Indian an entrepreneur rather than becoming a simple manager. A simple manager is one who just thinks, 'Okay, here are the people, here are the resources, here is the factory, and let me manage it.' And he manages somehow without much damage. That kind of management is outdated now. What we require is to look for opportunities. Opportunities are everywhere, grab them and offer your own unique solutions. You must make a difference. That kind of a talented team is to be built. Leadership talent is very important and the ability to think new, in different ways, is also very important. Old solutions will not work. We have to think of new solutions. We want to do things in different ways.

In a fluid and fast changing market, what is important is employability. That alone can work. A professor can become a fruit seller later. Why should a professor be a professor all the time? Fruit selling is also a complicated business these days. You need management research, market intelligence, people skills and a host of other abilities to do a simple business like fruit selling. At present our productivity is abysmally low. Every worker has to improve his productivity. Without improving individual productivity, improvement of the country's productivity is not possible. Why are Narayana Murthy and Azim Premji competitive? That is simply because they have gathered very productive people around them. They live and function in a very competitive and productive environment.

All knowledge workers are given a share in the company. So they all grow together. They participate in the company's growth. They are not exploited. They all are conscious of their rights in the company. This is how these companies grow. We need that kind of culture in our country, a very competitive culture.

In this competitive environment, people feel stressed. You are stressed because you have to satisfy your clients, and you have to maintain certain quality in a fast changing business scenario. As a result even a successful person, whether he is a manager or a leader, by the age of 40-45 is burned out. Either stomach problems or heart problems or kidney problems or family problems, all kinds of problems arise. On one side they are competitive and successful and on another side they have health, psychological and family problems. So they spend a lot of money on health issues. They say that in the world 50% of the people don't get sleep, because they don't have food. They go on an empty stomach to bed. Another 50% don't sleep, because they eat too much food. So both ways 100% are sleepless. The only country where people sleep a lot is in India! In other countries they spend millions of dollars on sleeping pills to get a wink of sleep. Here we can sleep anywhere, in the railway station, or on the road, or in the office room. As one wit said, 'in our office there are two classes of people- backward and forward!' Forward means people who sleep with their head on the table. Backward means people who sleep leaning on the chair. Then somebody said that in his office there is a third specimen- flat ward. They just lie down on the floor and snore away. So this is the kind of culture we are experiencing today. With this culture you cannot build a first class country or a first class economy competing with China, Europe and the United States of America.

If we want to build global corporations, if we want to become global business leaders, if we want to send our products all over the world, we have to become competitive. Look at China! China exports worth $ 800 billion dollars of merchandise while India exports only 70 billion dollars worth. That is a shameful situation. Both India and China started from the same position. China leaped forward but we are still at the old position. We have all the advantages. Ours is a very diverse nation and diversity gives you business competitiveness. For example, in Microsoft, 50% of the people who work there come from outside. Diversity gives them strength and brings new ideas. When you travel in India, you see incredible diversity. People in different regions have different facial features, different traditions, different cultural backgrounds, different eating habits; different dressing styles and they speak different languages. This diversity, a problem in the past, is considered an opportunity in the present. We can leverage diversity as business advantage. Our English speaking ability is an advantage. Though we speak English awkwardly, we can train our people to speak good English. Our educated middle class has learnt by rote the vocabulary and grammar. They just need a little polish. The modern world is going to be an English-speaking world; at least 50% of the world community is going to transact business in English. Our IT knowledge and computer skills are an advantage. You can leverage all these, provided you know how to pull yourselves together.

Emotional Intelligence

Our management students, instead of working in corporate anthills, must come out as entrepreneurs. They should do business and produce wealth on their own. It is this spirit that we have to teach the young Indians. Mere managers are not enough. They have to become leader managers so that they can build great companies and lasting organizations. It could be a small organization, but still they can build a niche for themselves. This is how we should think when we talk of managerial efficiency. But mere efficiency is not enough. What we have to build is effectiveness. Efficiency depends upon your academic qualifications. If you can manage a machine then you are an efficient person. It is easy to manage machines, but you need special skills to manage people. People are a critical asset in modern management. If you don't know how to manage people you cannot be an effective manager. You may be an efficient person with all the degrees from the best universities, but without being effective you will not be able to deliver. You will not be able to realize the goals and targets because you are lacking in mental and emotional skills. What you require in the modern world is not only analytical intelligence, what they call IQ, but you also need EQ, or emotional intelligence. EQ is the ability to manage your emotions in an interactive world.

Emotional intelligence is not part of the curriculum and is not cultivated in our universities. Your left side of the brain that deals with analytical intelligence is well developed, but the right side that deals with emotions is not developed. Unless modern managers acquire skills to manage their mental environment, they will collapse halfway through their career. Though successful managers, they will not be there long enough to enjoy success. We need this soft skill to manage our emotions, our health, our family and relationships in our effort to become competitive managers.

We Have To Be the Best

We have to be the best in the world. Not by cheating, but by hard work and creating value for the customer's money holding the philosophy that the customer is God. We have to create not just value but competitive value. Anything else is secondary. For achieving this objective, we the managers have to dedicate ourselves to the pursuit of excellence and quality.

12

Cross-cultural Values for Global Managers*

Verily, none remains inactive even for a moment; for all are forced to act by their inborn tendencies determined by gunas.

Bhagavad Gita: 3:5

I have been trying to share with you some of my thoughts that were inspired by my studies of the Indian wisdom tradition. I am also inspired by the dream that India can become a world power, economically, politically and culturally by 2020. India can also become a middle-income economy by that time. 'India Inc' is going to play an important and critical role in the world affairs. So we have a duty to prepare our people – our managers, our politicians, intellectuals and spiritualists, to take up this historic role. It is that spirit which animated me while I was designing these lectures.

The world has shrunk into a global community. India is also going global. We may act local, but we have to think global.

*Lecture delivered at All India Management Association (AIMA), New Delhi on 19th March 2004.

What is happening in India today is exactly the opposite- we think local and try to act global. That does not work; our ideas and mindset should become global. I had a very wonderful experience last year. I was called to talk to a group of managers in the Apple Industry in San Jose, USA, where they manufacture computers. I was not confident because they were all cutting-edge people. How would a *Swami* interact with them? I was ushered into a hall where about sixty people were sitting. I was purposely assessing the composition of the group. There were two Australians, two South Africans, three Malaysians, one Korean, and four Indians. The rest were white Americans. I found in that small room a melting pot of people drawn from different parts of the world. I thought that this represented the modern world. People from all over the world belonging to different cultures, traditions, belief systems, and races coming together to create a team to design and build computers. I thought that to be the pattern of the future. The world has become small and every workplace has become multi-cultural. We must develop psychological skills, attitudes, and paradigms to deal with this multi-cultural complexity and to manage diversity. Such skills are going to be of critical value for modern managers. If India wants to play a big role in the world, Indian managers must develop the ability to manage diversity.

The welcome point is that we have a great tradition of managing diversity. We are not new to this problem. Ours is a country where people speak different languages, belong to different religions, to different races, and come from different regions with different characteristics. For the past five thousand years India has been dealing with this problem of managing diversity. Today in the global workplace there is great diversity. In Microsoft 50% of their employees are non-Americans, with a large component of Indians. So is the case with IBM and NASA. The strength of an organization depends on its ability to invite and attract people from diverse backgrounds and then manage their aspirations, and that is going to be the trend of the future. We must feel comfortable with diversity, and have the ability to create consensus and to build teams out of diverse people and set goals and create solutions.

Take, for instance, a typical family. I was invited to a family in the USA. The lady of the house, an Indian, was married to a white Protestant American and that, too, a divorcee with three children. I was shocked. Of course it was my first visit to the States and thereafter you get used to such things. The eldest son is married to a Korean-Catholic, the middle one is married to a Japanese Buddhist and the third one is married to an Arab Muslim. I found the family has become multi-racial and multi-cultural. Similarly, workplaces also are becoming multi-cultural, and nations are becoming multi-cultural. America, Germany, France, and England are really multi-racial and multi-cultural nations. They are not helplessly but consciously becoming multi-cultural. What you require is an ability to attract the best from all over the world. You should know that talents are distributed very sparsely. You find some talent in India, some in South Africa, some in China, and some in Russia. There is no country where all the talents converge. You have to track talents all over the world. If a country fails to do that, it will die a slow death. That is what is going to happen perhaps to Japan, because they don't attract talents from the world. Some scientists predict that there will be no Japan in 3500AD because of the declining birth rate. That is what may perhaps happen to Russia, because they don't invite talents from other places. But in Britain, USA and other Anglo-Saxon cultures we find that they are comfortable with diversity. They even celebrate diversity.

Managing Diversity – The Indian Tradition

Being comfortable with diversity is an important value for the global leader. He must have the ability to understand different cultures and religions. He must be comfortable with Islamic tradition, the Hindu tradition, the Confucian tradition, the Christian tradition, the Sikh tradition, Buddhist, and Jain traditions. He should not feel alien to any tradition. Similarly, he should feel affinity to different styles of music— African music, Russian music, the classical music, and the rock music. And we have that tradition in India. India's central teaching is: *'Ekam sat viprah bahudha vadanti'*- truth is one but scholars describe and approach it differently. The Indian national motto is *'Nanatve Ekatvam'* – 'Unity in Diversity' or 'One in the Many,' whereas the American motto is, 'E pluribus Unum' – 'From the Many, One.' There is a difference in the metaphors they use to describe their national ideals. America uses the expression of a melting pot, whereas India uses the metaphor of a garland. A garland is a thread, which holds different flowers without destroying their individualities, whereas a melting pot cooks and mashes up all the vegetables into a soup.

Diversity has been there in the Indian tradition. Swami Vivekananda talked about it in the First Parliament of Religion in 1893 in Chicago and he got the longest ovation for that statement. It was said in the religious context, that God is one and you can approach God from many paths. Now, we are coming to a situation where we say that Gods are many as every individual is a potential God. If you nourish individuals you get a multitudinous flowering of Gods. Every worker will express himself in his own unique way; a garden with many flowers and colours, there will be an explosion of rainbows in your workplace. Just as biodiversity is important for survival of the human species, cultural diversity is also important for creative expression of human being because it challenges each other. You can worship God in the form of *agni*- fire, or in the form of *surya*- Sun, or in the form of your own *prana*-breath says the Rig Veda. So there are many ways of expressing and experiencing divinity. That idea has to be brought into the workplace. That idea has to become part of management ethos, and that is the Indian tradition.

The Indian tradition also says, '*vasudhaiva kudumbhakam: ayam nija paroveti ganana laghuchetasam udaracharitanam tu vasudhaiva kutumbakam,*' 'Thoughts of 'thine and mine' are the blemishes of small-minded people. For those who are large hearted, the whole world is one family' says the Hitopadeasa. Aphorisms like 'East is east and West is west and the twain shall never meet' are obsolete. The East nourishes the West and the West enriches the East. We all are at home whether we are in the East or in the West. If you are an Indian corporate leader with a global presence you must be traveling a lot. You could be sleeping in Delhi, eating your breakfast in Berlin, having an afternoon meeting in London and your dinner in New York. You must be psychologically prepared for that kind of a fast life, if you want to be a global leader. A modern manager must read the Bible, the Koran and the Bhagavad Gita, the Dhamma Pada, and also the Wealth of Nations. A leader cannot be parochial in his vision. He has to be multi-faceted and multi-cultural. In India we have this saying – *anno bhadra kratavo yantu visvatah* – let noble thoughts come from all sides. Every kind of thought or perspective is welcome. That has been a principle enshrined in the Vedas.

A global manager must also reckon with the fact that there may not be many social institutions to support him emotionally. In olden days you had intermediary institutions like family, church, temple or community or close friends, which gave you psychological support when you were down and out. In olden days when you came home with a big problem, your wife would be there with a cup of coffee and a smile. These days, modern liberated wives will not be there to receive you when you come home. They will either be in the club or pursuing their own careers. You cannot expect much support from your children, from the church, or from other civic groups. You are alone in the world on the top of the hill. You must have some inner reservoir of energy, without which you will not be able to cope with the challenges of modern management. This is expressed in the summit idea of the Indian tradition- '*tatvamasi*' – 'thou art that'. It is a wonderful idea. All that you aspire, whether it is health, energy, and happiness, you have to discover it from within yourself. Your consciousness is the ultimate center of values. The higher values that you seek are latent in your Self, in your own consciousness. Through contemplation, meditation and prayer and self-giving work you will be able to invoke energy and all those values from within yourself. There is no other source of support for the modern individual, because we are living in a world of rat race, the-dog-eats-dog world, where nobody will support you in your growth. We must be able to find resources from within ourselves. That is what *rishis* of India discovered long ago.

Let us see some of the values, which the Indian tradition speaks about. There is a verse in the *Bhagavad Gita* which says, '*yajna karma dana karma tapa karma na tyajyam iti cha apare.*' (Gita: 18.3). 'Actions in the form of self-giving work, sharing and austerity should not be relinquished.' What is the meaning of *yajnakarma*? *Yajnakarma* means socially productive activity. A modern manager has to be highly sensitive to the social, ecological and ethical issues. You cannot just think of your company and your profit only. Look at Enron. Enron was a high profile, mighty company, and within days, before your eyes, it exploded simply because of the unethical practices of the Enron management. Ethics has become an important survival tool in the modern manager's kitty. The second aspect about which a modern manager has to be sensitive is the ecological issue. Unless you incorporate the ecological factor into the management decisions, there will be no sustainable growth and profit for the company. This is what Bill Ford, the present Chairman and CEO of Ford motors, says to his executives.

Ahimsa as Core Value

The Indian tradition says that the world is one family; that you have to imbibe ideas from all sources. There are many paths to the same truth. Ultimately it all boils down to one value- tolerance or *ahimsa.* I find that the ideal of *ahimsa* will become a very important survival value for the modern manager. What do you mean by ahimsa? The Buddha, Mahavira and Mahatma Gandhi talked about *ahimsa.* Mahavira expounded a philosophical theory for *Ahimsa*. He called it *anaikantavada* or *saptabhangi nyaya*. *Saptabhangi nyaya* means that the same phenomenon can be understood in seven ways or studied from seven perspectives. *Anaikantavada* emphasizes the many-sidedness of truth. And hence no methodology or system of belief can claim absolute hold over truth, which makes us humble and prepares us to listen to the viewpoints of others.

Ahimsa means respect for dissent and disagreement. If someone agrees with you, he is not giving any additional value to you or your company because he is repeating whatever you already know. *Ahimsa* is not just non-killing. *Ahimsa* means the ability, the universality of mind, where you accommodate every dissent and difference. Celebrating difference is *ahimsa.* Different views, different philosophies, different attitudes, different perspectives, different needs are to be integrated and then alone you become a true person of *ahimsa*. Hitler was a vegetarian but that did not make him a good person. He was one of the most violent tyrants that the world has ever seen. Dalai Lama is a non-vegetarian, but that does not make him a cruel person. He is the holiest person that the world has at this point of time. *Ahimsa* does not mean you don't kill or hurt a mosquito. That is not the idea of *ahimsa*. *Ahimsa* means an ability to accommodate difference and dissent. You should not feel startled or offended when somebody disagrees very strongly with you. He may be your subordinate. You must encourage dissenting points of view. A leader who can encourage diversity alone can thrive in the modern world. That is what the American companies are doing. This kind of tolerance for difference may create a state of disequilibrium, ambiguity and ambivalence in your organization. But that alone can help you to remain a growing, learning and creative organization.

India has been able to manage diversity because of the principle of *ahimsa,* which the Buddha and Jainamuni propagated. Mahatma Gandhi was a great votary of *ahimsa*. In my earlier lecture I talked about the concept of *yajna*, where a group of people engage in constructive and creative work doing social good. *Yajna* is based on the concept of *ahimsa*.

The second principle, Krishna talks is *tapa karma*. *Tapas* means practice of austerity, or personal discipline. The problem with the modern managers is that they are over-indulgent people. Their idea is that the winner should take it all. If I am the winner, I must get everything. That makes you an overindulgent person. The more you indulge, the more inefficient you become. That is why at the age of 40, in spite of being successful and being on top of your company, most of the time you spend in the ICU. You develop backache, your kidney is weak, you have blocks in the heart, your lungs are malfunctioning, and you have started developing stomach ulcers. You were already suffering from diabetes and high blood pressure. You smoke and drink heavily and now you are chronically fatigued. This is not my definition of a successful manager, who is not able to hold himself together, a manager who commutes between the hospital and the corporate office. He has become dysfunctional at his most creative age! What a colossal waste of talent!

There should be some way of organizing personal life and

that is possible when you become an ethical person. *Ahimsa* is a very important value, *yajna* along with *tapas* are important values. As you go up in the hierarchy your needs should come down, and if you don't do that, your doctor will suggest it to you! Sir, give up sugar because you already have high sugar in the blood, don't take salt because your blood pressure is high and don't sleep on cushy bed and sleep on hard surface because you have got a back problem, don't use big pillows because you have got a spondylitis. Your doctor will force you to renounce all indulgences and practice *tapas*.

Learn to become a *Sanyasi*

Modern managers or top leaders should learn to become *sanyasins*. *A*ccording to Bhagavad Gita an important value for a successful person is *dana karma* – sharing. You must learn to share your resources. To share your resources you should have an inner sense of abundance. Otherwise you will not be able to share your resources. When you have that sense of abundance, because of your spiritual attitude, you will be able to share resources. So *yajna, dana*, and *tapa* are critical values which are to be practiced by the global manager. As you share, you expand your consciousness and you are able to draw more from the inner resources. 'To share is to grow, to possess is to perish'.

I would also like to refer to the ideas presented by Stephen Covey in his celebrated book, *Seven Habits of Successful People*. Let me talk about three out of his seven principles. One principle that he talks about is the idea of win-win situation. Nobody has to be a loser in the modern market place. Everyone has got a right to succeed. India and Pakistan need to learn from that idea.

Both India and Pakistan can be happy and successful countries if win-win situations are created. Another idea talked about by Stephen Covey is synergy. When two independent people come together or corporations collaborate, they can work in tandem and create extra energy. This is called synergy. What was hidden when you are independent will manifest when you collaborate and become interdependent. And when these companies work together for greater objectives what they generate is hynergy, an explosion of creativity.

In any relationship, we must have the patience to understand our counterpart. Most of the time, we don't have the patience whether it is in the family or in the corporate world. Half the way, before the other person completes a sentence, you cut into it. This inability to listen has become a major problem in the modern world. The modern manager must develop the patience and the capacity to listen to others. The more you listen the more you integrate and the more efficient you become. This is what Stephen Covey emphasizes, 'better understand than be understood.'

The *puranas* give description of *Lord* Vishnu who was supposedly a great manager. Vishnu is the *sthithi kartha*, the protector of the creation. Let me call him the chief executive of the world. He has got only a meager staff comprising one individual- Lakshmi, his consort. He has a driver called Garuda and his office is very sparsely equipped. There are no modern amenities in the office, only a couch. Most of the time, he reclines on the couch. He does not speak much. He watches everything, lying down on the couch in his little room and he doesn't interfere, for he knows that everything will function on its own.

That is the quality of a competent manager: he should not interfere, he must delegate, he must trust, he must find talent, and put the right people at the right place on the right job.

As a result Vishnu relaxes all the time. *Shanthakaram bhujagasayanam padmanabham suresham* – the meaning is, "always of pleasing disposition, reclining on the serpent couch, a lotus growing from his navel, the God of gods, Vishnu remains relaxed.' Only when a crisis comes he becomes active, like an emergency light. This metaphor is a perfect example of a highly competent and effective manager.

Stephen Covey says: 'Listen to others intently'. When you listen to other persons that way you help solve his problem. Listening capacity has to be cultivated. The word for listening in Sanskrit is *sravanam*, which is the foremost quality expected of a spiritual seeker. Covey talks about few more qualities for a successful manager, like 'pro-activity', 'first thing first', 'the ability to keep the whole in view' and 'keeping the sword sharpened', so that whenever you have to act, you don't have to look for the tool. It is ready by your side. The modern leader has to keep learning, and keep educating himself.

Daya, *Dana* and *Dama* – Compassion, Sharing and Self-Discipline

I conclude my talk with a story about Brahma. Brahma is the creator of the world. He created three creatures, humans, devils and Gods – *manava, danava, and, deva.* All the three are Brahma's mind-borne children. These three children of Brahma went to him and requested, 'Father, please teach us.' Brahma was very busy and in a hurry. He just uttered three words, '*da da da*,' and said, 'Go and meditate.' They understood the sound '*da*' in different ways in their meditation. *Asuras* are cruel people. They enjoy torturing others. They are sadistic and wish misfortune for others. The *asuras* reflected and thought that Brahma wanted them to practice *daya*, compassion, as an antidote to cruelty. Human beings in their meditation also thought about Brahma's teaching. They discovered that their problem was enormous greed and they were to practice sharing and giving, *dana*, as an antidote. *Devas* contemplated and realized that their problem was undue indulgence and they have to practice *dama*-austerity.

The three values that Brahma taught to his creation are *Daya*, *Dana* and *Dama*. The modern human has all negativities, which hinder him from realizing his spiritual potential. And hence we need to practise all the three values simultaneously. Without that you will not be able to integrate with the society, nor will you be integrated with your own self and become a successful manager.

T.S. Elliot, who got Nobel Price for his celebrated poem, *The Wasteland,* concludes his poem with these three Sanskrit words from the *Brahadaranyaka Upanishad.* They are: *dayadhvam*, *dattata, and damyata.* They successively mean, compassion, charity, and austerity. The world of management needs these ethical and humanistic values. Through that alone we will be able to build lasting and enduring organizations, create values for the customer and for humanity at large. After all, management deals with creation of value.

13

Indian Management for Global Competitivenss*

This is mine. That is theirs. Such thoughts belong to people of limited vision. Those who enjoy integral understanding know that the whole world is one family.

Hitopadesa

Competition and competitiveness are the two most important concepts in the world of management. Nature works on the law of competition. We are only adopting the law of nature into our social and institutional framework and in our economic and political interactions. Therefore an understanding of what is the law of competition, or how competition works, is very important for us in understanding human behavior and social interactions. If you look at nature, you find operation of the law of competition. The strongest and the fastest animal or the one that can best adapt to the environment survives in the forest. The same law we find operating in the human society. Any system, if it ignores this basic law of life, will not survive.

*Lecture delivered at All India Management Association (AIMA), New Delhi on 29th March 2005.

We have to situate whatever we are talking today on this iron clad law of competition and natural selection whether it is a spiritual principle or an ethical principle. The famous scientist Darwin expounded the law of survival of the fittest. We simply cannot ignore his findings. If we ignore that fact, then we will be living in an idealistic world and become a martyr or earn a place in the annals of history as a person who lived a highly idealistic life. But we will not be able to influence human behavior and create success in our lives. I believe that the law of competition or the principle of competition is a natural principle. We cannot deny it. All that we will discuss today is based upon that principle. The law of competition is one of my basic assumptions for today's presentation.

We Indians have something very basic to us that helps our survival. India has a very liberal tradition. We believe in and worship many Gods. We do not say that truth can be approached through one God or one window only. We believe that we can approach truth from many perspectives, many windows, and in many ways. Hence we have many traditions. We have the *Buddhist* tradition, the *Jain* tradition, the *Vedanta* tradition, the *Nyaya* tradition, the *Yoga* tradition, the *Kundalini* tradition, the *Tantric* tradition, and many more local traditions. Indians are comfortable with many ideas and even with many gods. In a typical Hindu *pooja* room, we find many gods smiling at us. *Krishna* is smiling, *Rama* is smiling, *Shiva* is smiling, *Ganeshji* is there, *Hanumanji* is there and the local gods and goddesses are also there. All the Gods are smiling at us and without an iota of jealousy among them. We are able to chant the mantras and offer oblations to the many Gods. It is said in the Bhagavad

(Gita: 4.2) *ye yathaa mam prapadyante tan tathaiva bhajamyaham mama vartamanuvartante manushyah partha sarvasha'* - 'in whatever form you worship me, in that particular form I will bless you. In all ways men walk in my path.' We have the freedom of worship. Our brain is wired to worship God in multitudinous ways. We feel more comfortable with the pluralistic worldview, and with difference and dissent.

In our effort to create an Indian management style, it is very important to position India in the global context. In such a scenario, we must have an Indian management style. Otherwise we will not be able to have that self-confidence nor will we have that ability to explore and express our potentialities. We have to develop an Indian management style just as they have an American, or a European or a Japanese style of management. After all, these styles are only different in expression. The ideas are the same. The Japanese use their own words, Americans use their words and we have to use our own words. There may not be much difference in ideas, because human behavior and character is almost universal. There are historical dissimilarities between people. Therefore, we have to use words and ideas which reflect our cultural tradition.

When we talk about Indian wisdom, let us not blindly accept whatever is there in our tradition. That is another fallacy we aught to avoid. Some people say that whatever is Indian is glorious. I don't subscribe to that belief. There is a lot of junk in the Indian tradition. We have to truthfully look at it and we have to accept only whatever is logical and useful. Winston Churchill said, 'Those countries that forget their past will have no future'. But I would like to rephrase that sentence: '*unless you create a future, nobody will care to remember your past'.* Your past is significant only if your future is significant. Therefore, more than remembering and getting lost in the past, what is necessary is to have a critical look into the past and remove the overgrowth and keep what is central and key to our wisdom tradition. An insider's critique of our entire past is long overdue. Great foreign Indologists such as Max Meuller, or Paul Dausen, may not be the right scholars to undertake such a critique. We alone understand the pulse of our culture. No doubt, Raja Ram Mohan Roy, and Swami Dayananda Saraswati did critique Indian traditions, but their voices are not heard much these days. It is very important that the Indian thinkers and religious teachers have that critical attitude, which is missing in the present discourse on the Indian cultural tradition. We all want to be politically correct. We don't want to criticize and don't want to touch the holy cow of Indian culture. Why we hesitate to critique Indian culture may be due to our undue self-doubt, a hangover from the colonial past. *We must have the courage and clarity to critique our past, interpret it and adapt those nuggets of wisdom to the needs of modern times.*

Pluralism is our Core Tradition

Let us look at the central ideas in the Indian wisdom tradition that may help us in creating an Indian management theory and management practice. The first idea is that truth is one, but wise men describe it differently. The Indian idea of truth is not monotheistic. In the Western tradition, there is only one God, one path, one savior and one myth. India is not comfortable with that kind of understanding of God and truth. We say there can be many Gods, many paths, many prophets, many books and many myths. Such an approach alone can unfold the meaning of truth and our own potentialities. In fact, there are as many truths as there are people. You all can have your own understanding of truth. That is why Indian mythology progressively raises the number of gods from 33 to 333, to 33 thousand and further to 33 million, and finally to infinity. You create your own truth. For an Indian, truth is an open space.

I find that modern management requires that kind of understanding of truth because our workplace is also very pluralistic. You find people coming from different religions, races and countries. You need a mindset to interact with all these people. Then alone you can create great organizations. And this truth is applicable to Indian blue chip organizations like Infosys, Tatas or Wipro. If they want to be great companies with a global presence, they have to draw talent from all across the world. A Hindu is comfortable working with staunch Christians, Muslims and atheists, but on the other hand people of those backgrounds may not be comfortable working with people of different faiths and cultures because of their monotheistic tradition. They believe in converting people of different faiths. We believe in including people with differences. They believe in flattening differences. We believe in encouraging differences. A mindset where you are comfortable with pluralism is important for survival in the 21st century. We cannot survive with a monotheistic mindset peacefully in the global village. I think the 21st century and the phenomenon of globalization belongs to pluralism. Pluralism is our tradition. The ability to manage diversity, to draw nourishment from diversity and use diversity as a means of discovering the truth, is part of Indian tradition. Discovering truth means unfolding our inner potentiality. Discovering truth is not a one-time event. It is an ongoing process. That is possible only when you live in diversity. Hence I think the 21st century belongs to the Indian wisdom tradition simply because of the fact that ours is a pluralistic culture.

The World is one Family

The second important aspect of Indian wisdom tradition is that we believe that the world is one family. A divisive attitude like 'this is mine' and 'that is yours' is not encouraged in the Indian wisdom tradition. We believe that everything belongs to God and that the whole world is one family. We may have little walls around us but we are always ready to stretch across the fence and shake hands with our neighbors. That is the friendliness we are taught in our tradition. The Vedas say, *mitrasya chakshusha ikshamahe*, 'May we see with the eyes of friendliness.' When I hear people say, 'Oh! India is opening up. Chinese are coming here. Americans are coming here. This is neo-colonialism.' I feel nauseated. It is absurd to say that opening up is an invitation to neo-colonialism. Colonialism happened because we were asleep. Now we are awake. Now India is no more an elephant; India is a tiger. The world has accepted the power of India. If you are alert, then challenges are good for you. If you are lethargic, then challenges are bad for you. This global competitive environment is good for us. It will help us unfold our latent potentialities. It will make India an enlightened nation. The whole world becomes an arena for us. '*Jagatrayam sambhava nartana sthali natadhirajotra parashiva svayam, sabha, nada, ranga, iti vyavastiti svarupata shaktiyutat prayuktah,'* meaning that the three worlds constitute the dancing stage. The dancer Shiva is our inner consciousness. The stage, the spectators and the dancers are all manifestations of this same consciousness.

Who is afraid of ideas coming from different directions? Only lazy people! Only people who are uncreative are afraid of the Chinese. I am happy that the Chinese are coming, because I get a good competitor. When I find a good competitor, I can bring the best out of me. Why should we be afraid of the Chinese or the Japanese or the Americans? Only a weak nation will be afraid of them. As Mahatma Gandhi said, 'Keep all the windows open, let the wind blow from all sides, but keep your feet planted on the ground, so that you are not swept off.' That is all we have to do.

Let us think ourselves as global citizens. India's future is centered on this understanding. We are rooted in India, but our branches can grow and give shade to the entire world. We are one, whether you are black, brown or white. In India we find all the colours and complexions, but we are comfortable with that. That is the second idea that we have to propagate to our Indian managers. Let all come here and let us all go over. That is the only way to grow and unfold our latent potentiality.

Meaning of Desire

The third idea that we have to draw from the Indian wisdom tradition is the meaning of desire. I find that in most of the spiritual discourses you are asked to put down desires - desire is evil, desire is the villain, and desire is the problem.

Therefore let there be no desires. Our young managers are all confused.

What are you talking? If there is no desire, there is no effort. If there is no effort, there is no creativity. If there is no creativity, there is no creation. And if there is no creation there is no management. And management is all about creating wealth. When you say that Indian tradition is against desire and the creation of wealth, you are cutting at the very root of the Indian wisdom tradition and a central management principle. After all, what is management? Is it not utilizing scarce resources to create maximum wealth? And you say desire is evil. That is the fallacy that India has been living with for the last 1500 years. On the contrary, when we read Indian scriptures, we find desire is the very source of creation. Even gods desire. The Taittiriya Upanishad says, 'God desired to become many and His expansion became the world.' '*Sokamayata bahusyam prajayeyeti...* '– He became many as a result of His desire to expand. He enjoyed all that he created and He entered into the creation and became many creatures. It is not that after creation, he ran away. And Krishna says, '*dharmavirudho bhuteshu kamosmi bharatarshabha,*' (Gita: 7.11), that 'He is desire which is not against the rules of *dharma*'; meaning that desire itself is not bad, provided it is not harmful to other beings. We all are engaged in fulfilling different levels of desires. Desires motivate us, and propel us. In our effort to fulfill our desires, we come together. When we come together, we create synergy. We have a better chance of fulfilling our desires and therefore *desire is not against the Indian wisdom tradition.*

If you say there should not be desire, then the whole economic activity comes to a grinding halt. Why should you act if you have become desireless? When we train our young people to become desireless, it will be a tragic day for India. Let us not take that path. Desire is very important. Desire expresses as *gyana shakti,* knowledge power, *ichcha shakti,* will power, *kriya shakthi,* action power. Together they are called *sankalpa shakti,* power of mind. Hence, we have to nurture desire and channel it to positive and productive pursuits. Gita also says, 'Those who only think about the object of their desire, without working for its fulfillment, are hypocrites'. (Gita: 3.6). Most of us are hypocrites. We are always jealous of America, simply because they are a prosperous nation. At the same time we say money has no value. And all of us want to go and park ourselves in America! If I ask any young man where he would like to live, he will say, 'Oh, I want to live and work in America'. Even Swamis want to go to America. They don't want to come back because there life is very comfortable and organized. You get rewards for your effort, you get recognition, and efficiency is appreciated. True, there it is a very competitive society. You feel challenged and you are on your toes all the time. Only the lazy and indolent find America unpleasant and unwelcoming.

There is no point in saying that you have no desire, while at the same time envying others who have fulfilled their desires. That is a very hypocritical stance. So, let us admit that we have desires and we have to work for their fulfillment. In your effort to fulfill your desires, you come in contact with others who are equally engaged in fulfilling their desires. There come the rules of *dharma.* The two fundamental characteristics of *dharma* are truth and non-violence, being honest in your dealings and not hurting others. You can be together and work towards the fulfillment of your desires provided you follow *dharma.* So, let us not kid ourselves by saying that India stands for 'desire-less-ness'. If India stands for desire-less-ness, we would not have created this great civilization. We created this great civilization because we had the burning desire. We had the desire to build; we had the desire to create. And when we stopped doing that, we stopped progressing and that was the beginning of our downfall.

When you do a *yajna*, you make offerings to please the Gods. At the end of the *yajna,* you make demands to Gods who are pleased by your offerings. The Yajur Veda intonates, "*vittam chame yasahchame lokahchame pasavahchame putrahchame...*' 'O Gods! Grant me wealth, grant me fame, grant me heaven, grant me cows, grant me progeny.' It is a long list of demands. That is OK. Our Gods are all rich. Vishnu is very rich. He has Lakshmi, goddess of wealth, with him. Shiva is very powerful. Parvati, goddess of strength, is always with him. Brahma is very knowledgeable. Saraswati, goddess of knowledge, is his consort. All our Gods put together is the supreme Brahman, the endless source of wealth, power, and knowledge. This is the Indian concept of God. When we strive for the fulfillment of desires, I would say, it becomes a spiritual experience, provided you have the right attitude and knowledge. Pursuing your desires in the outer world is the means of drawing out your inner potential. I would say that it becomes a *moksha* experience. *Moksha* means the freedom of unleashing your potentialities. That is the meaning of freedom; you create your destiny out of yourself. You unfold your power and the more you do that, the freer you are. It is not a state of desire-less-ness that we are championing, but it is a state of fullness. In that state of fullness, you are in a position to give yourself totally and unconditionally and the more you give, the more you discover your inner worth.

When we talk of desire-less-ness, what we actually mean is the desire to give unconditionally out of our inner affluence. The more you give, the more you have. That way you can discover yourself. That is the idea of desire-less-ness. For that, you have to be actively engaged in work. Hence the Indian wisdom tradition says that you have to be tirelessly active. This was Krishna's advice to Arjuna. Arjuna wanted to run away from the battlefield. He was under the notion that he has to be desire-less and for that he has to go to the Himalayas and meditate. Krishna said, 'No way, you have to be here and fight this battle, win this battle, and enjoy your victory. Take up your bow and arrow and I am with you. Be an agent of victory and not a servant of defeat. Enjoy the fruit of your labour.' Hence, let us disabuse ourselves of this notion of desire-less work. It is desire prompted work. But here, the desire is to share, not to grab. In fact I find people everywhere motivated by desire. But then, when I, a *swami*, say that I have a desire, they suspect me. Some people call me a *materialist swami*. I think that is a good compliment for me, because all our Gods are materialist Gods. They have wealth, power and knowledge and they use it too, very effectively.

In fact spiritualism without materialism is meaningless idealism. Success is in combining material pursuits with spiritual understanding. That is what the Indian tradition is all about.

You have to discover God in your daily life. This world is not away from God. It is said in Katho-Upnishad (11-1-10): '*yadeva iha tadeva amutrah...mrityoh sah mrityum gachati ya* eha *nanaeva pasyati.*' 'Whatever is here in the material world is there in the heavens. Those who see any difference between heaven and earth, they go from hell to deeper hell.' You can be here on earth, open your wisdom eye and see God everywhere. Whoever creates division between spirituality and materialism, between God and the world, between soul and the body, is not being true to the Indian wisdom tradition.

Detached Engagement

When you are engaged in activity, then alone you can enjoy spirituality. It is creative effort that brings out your potential. We enjoy divinity in creativity. Hence Isavasya Upanishad says: '*Kurvan eva iha karmani jijivished shatam samah,*' (sloka 2). 'May you live 100 years of productive life.'! But the *rishi* cautions that to be creative is to renounce attachment to work and its results. And the *rishi's* advice is to 'Renounce and rejoice, detach and engage.' *Tyaktena bhunjitha (*Ishopanishad:sloka- 1*).* Work gives you dignity and purpose in life and an active life is a healthy life. Through such engaging work alone such realization of self is possible. That is how spirituality and management interests converge. Without that convergence there will be a gaping chasm between life and spirituality.

In order to highlight the idea of spirituality-management convergence, I have designed a new slogan, '*Goal realization is God realization.*' I find most of our management leaders are spiritually inclined people. They do *poojas,* they go to temples like Vaishnov Devi, Tirupati, and Guruvayur. But when it comes to management, they think spirituality has nothing to do with it. They think that management is a dirty practice, economics is a dismal discipline, and politics is a vicious game. This kind of a division in our consciousness has created conflict in our thinking and practice and that is the root cause of modern dilemmas. Very few people are able to live in harmony. Even those who are making efforts to harmonize spirituality with their daily life have doubts of their own. They fear that they may draw the right lessons from spirituality. They hesitate to give new and practical meaning to their spiritual experience. The Upanishads say, 'Fear is the road to death. Fearlessness is immortality.' – *'Abhayam vai Brahmaa'*, (*Brihadaranyaka Upanishad, 4-25)*.

Nishkama Karma – Renouncing Reaction

Finally, what is the meaning of *karma-yoga* or *nishkama karma*? *Nishkama karma* is defined very well in Gita. It means non-reaction to the fruits of work, or renouncing reaction to the fruits of work. Please note, renouncing reaction, not action. Your work does produce results, and according to the theory of *karma* you alone will receive the fruits of your work. The quality of your life does not depend upon the results of your work, but the attitude with which you receive them. Let me illustrate it with an example. When the baby son kicks you on the ribs, you enjoy it and appreciate the playfulness of the baby. Whereas when the same baby grows up and becomes a teenager and even hints at kicking you on the ribs you take it as an act of rebellion. The action remains the same. You interpret and experience it differently. The real fruit of the action is the interpretation of the experience, not the fruit itself. Depending upon the interpretation you suffer or enjoy the fruits. And interpretation is a function of knowledge and attitude.

Another consequence of reaction to the fruits is that you will not be able to improve upon your work. If you don't react you can learn from your failures and improve upon your successes. Therefore, *nishkama karma* is not action without desire, but is action without reaction to the fruits. And non-reaction is not total indifference, but appropriate response or controlled response. Krishna advocates, 'Mental poise in success and failure.' Indian managers have to understand the true meaning of *Nishkama karma*, which is a very powerful tool of unfolding your creative potentiality.

Follow your Bliss

Finally Krishna says, "Follow your bliss." All religions say, 'Do, as I say or to hell shall thou go.' But the Indian wisdom tradition says, 'Think for yourself and do as you wish'. This means that ultimately the responsibility rests on you. You are responsible for the choices you make. And life unfolds as a series of choices. You can consult everyone, but you alone have to process all the information based upon your life goals and ambitions and your innate dispositions and talents, and make decisions and own up responsibility for your decisions. That is the way to grow and unfold your potential.

So friends, if you can practice all these ideas given in our scriptures, the *Gita*, the *Upanishads*, *Vedas*, *Darshanas*, it should help you to become responsible citizens, competent managers, and great leaders. In the process, India can become one of the greatest nations in the world, rich in culture, values, knowledge, and wealth. Affluence is not opposed to spirituality.

help you to become responsible citizens, competent managers and great leaders. In the process India can become one of the greatest nations in the world rich in culture, values, knowledge, and wealth. Affluence is not opposed to spirituality.

EPILOGUE

14

Ten Spiritual Principles of Indian Management

Arise! Awake! Stop not till the goal is reached. Life is a delicate balancing act on the razor's edge.

Kathopanishad: 3:14

1. Indian worldview is fundamentally pluralistic. It accepts different perspective and narratives of reality as equally valid representations. This is reflected in the Vedic dictum: '*ekam sat viprah bahudha vadanti*' – truth is one but the wise describe it differently.

There are two world-views vying for world dominance – one polytheistic or pluralistic and the other monotheistic or monistic. Pluralism accepts differences and dissents as normal human behavior and is inclusive of all perspectives. Monism resents difference and diversity and is exclusive. Different cultures offer differing narratives of truth and each makes absolute claims on truth. The Jews, Christians and Moslems have their exclusive versions of truth. The Buddhists, the Jains and the Confucians have their own ways of knowing and expounding truth.

Hinduism, being a compendium of truth, has evolved a method of discourse for co-existence between believers of different faiths.

Hinduism is essentially a culture of co-existence and a mindset of inclusion. Monism and monotheism is a culture of coercion and conversion. Religious violence, terrorism, colonialism and slavery are natural consequences of monotheistic exclusivist claim. Science is another manifestation of a monistic mindset. It makes claim based on a certain methodology – observation and experimentation – that does not tolerate alternate and differing paradigms and assumptions. Science has no way of accommodating ethics and spirituality; aesthetics and imagination; emotions and fantasies. The whole world of beauty, values and meaning is beyond science. The Hindu and Confucian wisdom traditions emphasize the subjective with the objective and the importance of balance between them. The scientific tradition after Descartes ignored the subjective in its one-sided pursuit of the objective. A healthy science will be much humbler and more inclusive, and position itself beside other knowledge systems.

The Vedic statement that, truth is one but descriptions vary, captures the spirit of diversity, coexistence and the nonviolent mode of discourse, and it also reflects the dilemmas and contradictions of the complex world of modern management.

2. Indians are oriented towards globalization, though they are fiercely patriotic. They like to situate themselves in the global context. This spirit is reflected in the statement '*vasudhaiva kutumbakam*' – that the world is one family.

From times immemorial India has been the cross road between the East and the West. Greeks, Persians, Chinese and Arabs, and later Europeans came here and set up business and trade; propagated their faiths; taught their languages; and influenced Indian thinking. India is essentially a composite culture. In India we find a cross-section of all racial types – the yellow, the white, the black, the brown, and their unique blend of hues. Languages, customs, traditions and faiths overlap in the salad bowl of Indian culture. Boundaries fade, definitions constantly change, and what we get is an ever-shifting rainbow of colours and a soaring symphony of sounds, and a mouth-watering riot of tastes and nerve tickling sensations. India is a moving collage of a million creations. China is 93% Han, Europe is overwhelmingly white Christian. But India, though 85% Hindu, is a universe of distinct identities. Hence India does not think in terms of 'us' and 'them'. Because races and clans; gene pools and bloodlines have blended indistinguishably in this culture so that separation and exclusion is almost impossible. Hence, India came to this wonderful attitude that humans belong to one family with all their differences. It is not solidarity of faith, habit or speech. But it is solidarity of acceptance, synergy of opposites, win-win attitudes, leveraging strengths, a harmony of hearts, based on common interests and aspirations beyond ethnic and linguistic differences.

This saying from Hitopadesa reflects the Indian attitude pretty well – 'the whole world is one family'.

3. Indians regard the material world as an expression and an inalienable part of the spiritual reality. Hence they have a healthy respect for nature and all living forms. This attitude is expressed in the Vedic statement: '*sahasra sirsha purushah sahasraksha sahasra pad*,' that 'God exists with thousand heads, mouths, eyes and ears, hands and legs ... incarnate as the whole world'.

This is the Vedic standpoint that India still holds sacrosanct, that the visible world of time, space and events is the apparent form of the timeless, space-less, blissful consciousness – that is Brahman/God. Since it is a manifestation of God the world is also divine. Modern physics says that the material world is a modification of energy – a dance of atoms. Quantum physics is knocking on the door of consciousness in its enquiry into the heart of matter. All these developments point to the Indian view that the visible world is an expression of the invisible spiritual reality.

The Indian is a natural environmentalist. Love and respect for nature springs from this spiritual vision that all manifestations are parts of God – the rivers, mountains, oceans, air, fire, sky, clouds, plants, forests, cells and the brain. A Hindu is obligated to plant seven trees for the one that he fells. Hindu women go around the banyan tree for the blessing of conception. They plant and protect basil tree for the well being of their family. For the Hindu, the river Ganga is *Ganga mata,* the cow is *gomata,* and the home land is *Bharat mata*. One of the oft repeated Hindu morning prayers acknowledge the sanctity of the planet earth – '*samudra vsane devi parvata stana mandale vishnupatni namastubhyam padasparsam kshamasva me*' – 'O Goddess Earth, thou are draped by the blue oceans, your bosoms are the mountains, thou are the consort of Vishnu, please pardon the impertinence of putting my feet on you'. This tiny planet is our only home. Its health is entwined with humanity's health. Clean air, fresh water, and fertile soil, adequate forest covers are all indispensable for human survival. Planet earth is our nurturing mother.

The corporate world with its culture of consumerism has depleted world forest cover, exhausted hydro-fossils, polluted rivers and air, and poisoned the soil. Globalization of this destructive aspect of corporate culture should not be encouraged in the name of open market, world trade and economic development. Ecological sensitivity should be the highest form of business ethics. The developmental model that India chooses to incorporate ecological values will become the global model of development. The Indian understanding of the world as the body of God gives modern corporate community a spiritual basis for ecological concerns.

4. Indians consider the material world to be a constant flux and change and full of contradictions and paradoxes. Hence they welcome and appreciate change as a fundamental reality of nature. This vision is indicated by the Vedic concept of *maya* and the dictum: '*charaivedi charaivedi* – keep going'.

Change is the law of nature. Nothing remains the same. There is a Latin saying '*omnia mutantur nihil enterit*' – everything changes but nothing is lost. Since nature is manifestation of *Brahman*, the pure consciousness, change becomes the core reality of *Brahman*. But there is no depletion in reality because of these changes. The theory of conservation of matter explains this concept very well. The Isavasya Upanishad says 'infinite remains infinite in spite of any number of infinites taken out of the infinite.' Here a question arises that how can infinite be separated from infinite. Sankaracarya called this phenomenon *mithya* or *vivarta,* which means that manifested infinite is just an appearance. Gaudapada explained it as *ajata* – a non-event. Modern physics says that the quantum field is of infinite possibilities.

The world of time, space and events is full of contradictions and paradoxes. Each phenomenon gives rise to its own opposite. Life is a complex of constant change, is heterogeneous and hierarchical. In life everything is food for everything else.

This vision is most appropriate to the modern world of management. Corporations are complex structures riddled with contradictions that generate their own negations and opposites. The modern manager has to learn to live with all that and still deliver, keep deadlines, maintain quality, expand market share, innovate products, anticipate every move of his competitor and continue to grow to stay alive and afloat.

The manager also has to reinvent himself as he moves on, update his knowledge base, vision and technological skills. Management has to work for incremental changes in organizational structure, production process and use of human resource. The entrepreneur has to restrain his avaricious nature and function within ethical and ecological norms. The modern manager has to discover in him the Hindu trinity – Brahma, the creator, Vishnu, the sustainer and Shiva, the destroyer. This exercise becomes an endless process of creativity, a tireless pursuit of excellence, till he goes up in a flash of flames with his boots on. For a modern manager rest is rust. He has to remain as the silent, still center of the raging storm.

5. Indians consider that wealth and prosperity are created by a joint enterprise of give and take between gods, nature and humans. This is known as the *yajna* culture that is indicated by the Gita statement '*saha yajna praja srshtva purovaja prajapati anena prasavishyadhvam esha vaha astu ishta kamadhuk*' – having created human beings with *yajna* impulses Prajapati said 'May

you flourish through the *yajna* culture for *yajna* is verily *kamadhenu,* the wish fulfilling cow'.

It is trade and not aid that is the road to prosperity. Nations leverage their core competencies and produce and sell what they are good at, and buy and consume what is available at competitive prices in the market. Thus China exports manufacturing goods, India exports information technologies enabled services, and the United States export financial, insurance, accounting, legal services and high-end technologies. Thus, they fuel growth in all the three countries. On the other hand, countries trying to become self-sufficient by raising walls of protective tariffs have all become poorer and poorer.

The philosophy of *yajna* supports the concept of international trade. In the *yajna* resources are pooled and offered at a higher altar and blessings are received from Gods in return such as cattle, victory in battle, fame, progeny, heavenly joys etc. Gods, according to the Vedas, live on the offerings made by humans in the *yajna*. Fire carries those offerings to the respective Gods like Indra, Varuna, Surya and Marut. The empowered Gods send blessings in terms of rain, cattle, victory, etc. Prosperity is the result of this mutual nourishing and cherishing.

The *yajna* culture, a culture of dedicated teamwork in search of excellence and prosperity, is native to the Indian tradition. Organizations that follow the *yajna* style of work grow to become *kamadhenus* – wish fulfilling, achieving, growing, learning organizations. The *yajna* culture says that work is the best offering, team work brings out the best in individuals; that a team is made up of people of diverse talents who bring out their individual competences in a competitive environment while following the law of the land and rules of the game.

Such teamwork is offered at the highest altar that is customer satisfaction, quality products, innovative processes, competitive prices, after sale services, so on and so forth – to create an enduring and great company. The various aspects of the *yajna* culture are: (i) individuals with intellectual, practical and emotional skills, that is, well rounded workers, (ii) teams made up of those well rounded individuals, (iii) *yajamana* and *patni* – the entrepreneurs who organize the *yajna*, (iv) priest – managers and the CEO, (v) the three fires – production, finance and marketing, (vi) mantras – technology and processes, (vii) Gods – vision, mission and objectives, (viii) results – products, goods and services, (ix) balance after sharing with stakeholders – profit, (x) *kamadhenu* – great corporations that practice *yajna* culture and make huge profits

It is high time that Indian management adopted the *yajna* model of organizing corporations and created the *yajna* mode of teamwork and work culture. Then the Indian corporations will grow to become transnational *kamadhenus*.

6. Every human being is an infinite resource. Hence the greatest wealth is the human resource – the power of consciousness and knowledge. This truth is expounded in the Vedanta statement: *Tattvamasi* - 'thou art that' and *Sivohum* – 'I am Shiva'

We find two great movements in the philosophical thought of Indian tradition. One represented by Vedas and the other by Vedanta. The Vedic masters using the power of mantras and performance of rituals seek to control the forces of nature and Gods and secure worldly and otherworldly possessions and comforts. It is basically an extroverted materialistic project. Whereas the Vedanta masters through a process of cultivating inner values like prayer, detachment and meditation tried to attain inner bliss and spiritual powers. The slogan of the Vedas was *pravrtti* or extroverted activity and that of Vedanta is *nivrtti* or introverted activity. It is in the Bhagavad Gita that we find the harmony of these two pursuits, which is *nivrtti* in *pravrtti*. This new path inaugurated by the Gita is called detached activity or *nishkama karma*. It is beautifully explained in the Bhagavad Gita by a very telling phrase *karmani akarma darsanam* – remaining inwardly still and yet supremely active. This is possible because of the spiritual vision that every individual is essentially a field of infinite potentialities. This potentiality is called *Brahman* or limitless consciousness. *Brahman* being so full, expresses itself through creative enterprises. Every creative individual becomes a channel for *Brahman's* creative expression. When Vedanta says '*tattvamasi*' it means every individual has infinite potential. This potential is manifested through desire prompted activities. When desires are self-seeking, they block the expression of the infinitude of the self. On the contrary when desires are self-giving and altruistic they open up the wellsprings of inner creativity.

The modern management theory also says that the individual is the ultimate resource. The source of innovation is individual imagination and creativity. It is innovative products that add values to the customer's money and increase the profitability of the company. Modern management is interested in tapping into the mental and spiritual resources of individuals. An inspired worker with adequate sense of self-worth and inner happiness alone can add value to his work. Wealth is no more confined to natural resources, capital and technology. Wealth is in aesthetic beauty, environmental protection and ethical conduct. These soft sides of business will contribute increasingly to the concept of wealth and overall wellness. The world of management can benefit a lot from the vision of the *rishis* that human beings are essentially spiritual and sources of infinite creativity.

7. The theory of *karma* is fundamental to the Indian view of human action and its consequence. The *karma* theory says that every individual by his moment-to-moment choices become creator of his or her destiny. This shows the power and creativity of individual choices. The theory of *karma* is based on the logical proposition that the effect is a modification of the cause –'*karya karanayoh abheda*.'

The theory of *karma* is unique to the Indian wisdom tradition and is shared by Buddhists and Jains. It seeks to explain human experiences in terms of cause and effect. Human beings alone have the faculty to discriminate between right and wrong actions. With that knowledge humans are able to avoid wrong actions and perform right actions in his pursuit of fulfilling natural desires. Animal acts are based on instincts. If a deer jumps across a highway and is hit by a speeding car, it does not think that the resultant suffering is caused by its previous action. It just suffers and dies. But a human being judges his actions by their direct consequences or intended consequences. As individuals human beings enjoy freedom of choice unlike an inert object like a sword or a gun, which is only an instrument in the hands of the possessor. If with a sword you cut somebody's neck, it is not the sword that is punished but the wielder of the sword. The *karma* theory holds that every individual is free to make choices and is responsible for the actions he does. Thus he feels responsible for his present state of being and also for his future. By moment-to-moment choices and actions every individual creates his own destiny. The theory of *karma* empowers every individual and liberates him from external conditions as far as his future is concerned.

The modern management which believes in the power of reason and collective human action in controlling and changing human environment in order to create desirable outcomes can learn a lot from the empowering theory of *karma*.

8. Indians believe that the world is to be enjoyed and it can be enjoyed only if the enjoyer develops dispassion and detachment. This is indicated by the Upanishadic statement *tenetyektena bhunjita* – 'therefore, renounce and enjoy'.

According to the dualistic thinking, the world is full of evil and human beings are born sinners. Their sojourn on planet earth is brief and, as a result, a curse for disobedience, given by God. After creation, it is also believed that God commanded humans to enjoy the world. This belief caused the Western world to exploit nature recklessly by indulging endlessly in desire-fulfilling activities. The result is there for all of us to see – A situation where 3% of world population enjoys 27% of world resources causing 23% of world pollution. It is horrific to think of the tragedy, if this profligate life style is extended to 6.5 billion people of the world. On the contrary the Indian wisdom tradition believes that the world is an extension of God and human beings are his manifestations in the world. The Isavasya Upanishad says: 'Even the minutest speck of matter is enveloped and enlivened by God'. Hence, for the Indian, being in the world and enjoying the world has a different flavor altogether. It is like the relationship that exists between the child and the mother. When the child is breastfed by the mother she feels joyous and the child gets nourishment. To enjoy the world requires extreme personal discipline of the body, mind and the intellect. Enjoyment involves aesthetic pleasure, intellectual clarity, emotional fulfillment, and philosophical reflections. Enjoyment is more in terms of a life of harmony with nature. This inner joy is a function of not just sensuous pleasure gained by eating and indulging but by detached engagement and observation. The pleasure that we get by watching a moonrise or a verdant valley or a flock of geese in flight or a silken fabric woven by a firefly in the darkness of night is much more than all the pleasures that we get from physical indulgences. Enjoyment should not lead to enslavement and physical fatigue and illnesses. That is why the Upanishad says 'renounce and rejoice'; 'detach and enjoy'.

The modern manager for the sake of his personal health as well as for the health of the world may well practice this teaching of the Indian wisdom tradition.

9. Indians believe that no individual can avoid work. What gives fulfillment is not result of work but the very process of working and hence the Gita dictum 'enjoy work without reacting to the fruits of work' – '*karmanyevadhikaraste ma phaleshu kadachana*'.

Work, according to Indian wisdom tradition, all through from the Vedas, Upanishads, Dharmasastras, Bhagavad Gita and down to the philosophers and leaders of the freedom struggle of 20th century, is looked upon as the fundamental nature of human beings and the most authentic statement about his individuality. Nobody can avoid work without diminishing his self-worth, says the Bhagavad Gita. But work also creates social and psychological tensions. The Bhagavad Gita divides work into three stages: first the process of work, second expectation of result of work, and third, enjoyment of the fruits of work. It is the expectation of the fruits, which is a psychological process that causes the tension. Work itself does not cause tension. Nor does outcome create tension. It is the expectation that causes tension and stress. So the question is not how to avoid work, which is impossible, or how to avoid results of work, which is illogical. The question is how to avoid reaction, tension and stress. It is possible to avoid tension by changing ones way of thinking and keeping in mind the larger picture. Work one has to do, but one has no control over the outcome of work. Even if one is able to control the outcome of work there is no guarantee the outcome of work will result in giving fulfillment to the worker. The Gita separates the fruits of work and their enjoyment from real fulfillment. Real fulfillment is a self-referral value. The Gita admonishes, 'Don't work for enjoyment, but find enjoyment in work'. If one can continue to work joyfully one can make work a pursuit of excellence, beauty and goodness.

In modern management motivating people to work is the key challenge. No amount of rewards or awards or recognition will motivate the worker to work on a sustained basis to bring out his best potential. Management Gurus have lately discovered the worker has to be motivated by his own sense of work ethics or by making work itself a source of joy. In this context, Gita's analysis of work and the recommendation that work is to be undertaken without regard to personal reward becomes very meaningful. Once a worker knows that enjoyment is not in the result but in the very process of work, he will be psychologically and philosophically prepared to undertake work as a master does his own work rather than a slave who works for others.

10. Indians believe that *moksha* – individual growth, and *lokasamgraha* – common good, are complementary pursuits. This is indicated by the Gita statement : '*karmaaieva hi samsiddhim astita janakadayah lokasamgrahmevapi sampassyan karma kartum arhasi* – in olden days great kings like Janaka and Asvapathi gained spiritual realization through performance of their kingly duties of serving the people, protecting the weak and punishing the wicked. Therefore you also work tirelessly for the good of the world!

The perceived dichotomy between spiritual and material pursuits is because of a wrong conception of the relationship between God and the world. World is God's epiphany. God has created the world as a field for human beings to explore their minds, to purify their thoughts, and realize their potential and unfold their fullness through interaction with the world. True spirituality is being in the world without losing the self. From the Vedanta perspective, worldly activities are not opposed to spiritual pursuits. In fact, worldly activities are the only means of attaining spiritual fulfillment. The spirit is not a goal to be attained in the future by undergoing either transformation or transcendence. The spirit is an already established reality and the very heart of human existence. It is to be realized, as ones own self, by a process of awakening and not to be attained through time consuming activities. Hence the Gita says 'realize the self and serve the world'. Such altruistic activities become a means of unfolding ones potentialities.

This is a four-stepped growth

* First, one has to discover one's *svadharma* considering one's mental disposition, training and place in the society.

* Second, one performs svadharma with an attitude of surrender, which purifies the heart enabling access to the spirit.

* Third is realization of spirit as one's true nature.

* Fourth is manifesting that spirit through self-giving altruistic work.

Thus, Indian wisdom tradition combines worldly activities with spiritual pursuits. This is illustrated by the great metaphor in the Mahabharata where Arjuna was asked to hit the bird's eye by looking at the reflection of the bird in the surging waters. The eye of the bird represents the spirit. The surging waters indicate the turbulent world; reflection of the bird stands for the goals that we seek in the world. The bow represents a disciplined body-mind. The arrow represents supreme concentration. The metaphor says while you are working in the world fulfilling your worldly goals you will simultaneously be able to realize your spiritual targets by having the right attitude and vision.

The Indian managers coming from a seven-thousand-year old wisdom tradition are torn between the materialistic values of the industrial age and the spiritual values of the native culture. On one side they are asked to produce wealth. On another side, they are told that wealth is evil. On one side they are asked to promote the culture of consumption. On another side they are told that indulgence is the cause of down fall. This kind of a cleavage in perceptions leaves chasms in their soul. They become hypocritical and confused. They secretly go to temples, perform pujas, consult astrologers, but publicly they act as champions of secular humanism, rational thinking and material progress.

The Indian management has to address this issue by interpreting spirituality and redefining the concept of development. That is the task which thinkers of Indian management have to seriously address. I believe that the Indian wisdom tradition, which is holistic, sees no conflict between spiritual fulfillment and material progress. Liberation or *moksha*, which is the highest value in the Indian wisdom tradition, is not attained in the other world after death, but is the summit experience that a living individual experiences in terms of unfolding his potential through moment-to-moment choices, while interacting with the world.